Arcade Reflections

Memories of The Arcade in Dewsbury

The Arcade Group Dewsbury

Written and edited by Michael Mawson, on behalf of The Arcade Group Dewsbury

Acknowledgements

Many thanks to everybody who shared their memories of The Arcade with me. Special thanks to Josephine Ripley, Gerald and Janet Pearson, Maureen Crawshaw, David Blackburn, June Sykes, Richard and Ivor Burns, George Alexander, Steve Seller, Richard Bott, James Clow, Ruth Tolson, June Carter, Val Sheard, Sam Hirst, Malcolm Hirst, Ann Marie Firth, Deborah Wood, Sue Broadbent/Woodcock, Kath Savage, Jan Thwaites, Maggie Green and Judith Wood MBE. Thanks also to Margaret Watson and David Gaunt for valuable information and for permission to use their resources.

Many thanks to my early readers Helen Thom, Hilary Nicholson, Judith Mawson, Helen Connor, Al Rhodes, Nick Child, Dave Sharp and Pete Vivian – your comments, contributions and corrections were invaluable. Thanks to Lin White for formatting and for much sound advice in this area. Find Lin via coinlea.co.uk. Special thanks to Al Rhodes for cover design.

The research for this book was conducted during the Development Phase of Kirklees Council's bid to National Lottery Heritage Fund for funding to restore and reopen The Arcade in Dewsbury. Kirklees Council received a grant to deliver a range of activities during the Development Phase, one of which was the creation of an archive of historical material related to The Arcade, a process which resulted in the production of this book.

Huge thanks to Heritage Fund for making this possible.

Contents

Part One
1789 and all that!

1

&

French Lessons

1790-1815

Unlikely as it sounds, the story of The Arcade in Dewsbury starts on the filthy streets of late eighteenth century Paris. The streets of the French capital were notoriously dirty and dangerous. The only drainage was a narrow gutter in the middle of the street, supposedly designed to carry water to the already polluted Seine. However, in heavy rains these gutters became swollen and impassable. In the absence of effective drainage, the streets were regularly reduced to a sea of mud. To make matters worse, those citizens brave enough to navigate the grimy arteries of the great city on foot had no choice but to take their chances against an ever-increasing level of worryingly unrestrained horse-drawn traffic. New transport options, most notably the smaller, lighter (and subsequently significantly faster) two-wheeled gigs and cabriolets were especially threatening. These twin problems were compounded by a third, seemingly negligent oversight – the almost

9

complete absence of pavements.

The events which eventually led to this intolerable situation belatedly being addressed took place in a seemingly unrelated but equally dirty arena – politics. The French Revolution of 1789-99 convulsed the nation. An in-depth analysis of the social and political implications of those tumultuous years is perhaps not necessary here. For our purposes, it is sufficient to recognise that the old world of all-powerful monarchy, nobility and clergy was swept away. It was replaced by a brave new world of liberty, equality and fraternity, expressed most passionately by the growing class of increasingly wealthy merchants, traders, bankers, businessmen and lawyers.

Late eighteenth-century Paris was thus a city of contrasts. Fans of French period drama will be familiar with the sophisticated fashions of the time, exemplified by extravagant wigs, lace-trimmed suits and white stockings. Urban socialites were desperate to exhibit their newly acquired wealth and to flaunt their staunchly held political beliefs, preferably in a suitably cultured, refined, elegant public setting. In short, the country was hurtling rapidly towards the modern world. The streets, however, were still mired in the middle-ages, with shoe cleaners plying their trade on every corner.

The recently empowered upper middle classes were compelled to act. A number of factors informed their actions. Firstly, there was a desperate need for public spaces that were not only free from mud and standing water but also undisturbed by traffic and the worst ravages of the elements. Secondly, new marketing possibilities were needed for the burgeoning luxury industries that were nourished by the growing class of 'nouveau riche'. Shopping for pleasure, and what we would now call 'window shopping', had become popular leisure pastimes for the more sedate amongst the upper middle classes, and spaces to indulge such pleasures were in desperately short supply. Thirdly, plenty of real estate was available in the city centre, largely due to the post-revolutionary expropriation of property from the dramatically enfeebled nobility and clergy. And lastly, and perhaps most interestingly, under the new liberal legal arrangements, those few building regulations that did exist applied merely to the façades of buildings, thus enabling a greater degree of freedom with regards to the design and construction of internal structures.

There was an obvious response to this combination of factors – the construction of arcades. The first arcade was thus built in Paris, at the famous Palais Royal. Completed around 1790, it took the form which would soon become recognised as the classic design: covered, illuminated from above and with a row of shops on both sides. More importantly, it was the first public space removed from the disturbance of traffic.

Adopting the name 'Galeries de Bois', the Palais Royal arcade was quickly established as a popular city attraction, drawing a large and diverse crowd every day and an even larger and more diverse crowd at night. The appeal soon spread, drawing tourists from across

Europe. Visitors were drawn by the novelty of the new, by the magic of unfamiliarity, by the originality of this new fusion of the interior and the exterior (even today, in some of the larger arcades, it difficult to tell whether you are inside or outside).

The final few years of the eighteenth century saw the fashion for arcades adopted enthusiastically across the city, the Passage du Caire, the Passage du Panoramas and the Passage Delorme all opening their gates in quick succession. The architect and builder Monsieur Delorme is often considered the inventor of arcades, his perhaps being the first arcade to boast a continuous glass roof, a defining feature.

1815-1840

The first six arcades in the world were in fact built exclusively in Paris, all constructed by 1811. However, in the following decade or so no further arcades were opened in France. At the time the nation was absorbed in the tail end and aftermath of the Napoleonic Wars, as well as being victim of a wartime continental blockade. Ironically, these were the years during which at least one French export arrived on foreign shores.

The first arcade in Britain, the Royal Opera Arcade, opened in London in 1818. Sporting a single row of shops and a series of unusual round skylights, it was inspired by the style of a Turkish bazaar and became the blueprint for a uniquely British version of the arcade. The following year witnessed the opening of the Burlington Arcade. Less than a mile away from its neighbour, the Burlington incorporated a glass roof construction similar to that of the Passage des Panoramas in Paris. A third non-Parisian arcade, the Passage de la Monnaie, opened in Brussels at the end of the decade.

Recovery from the ravages of the Napoleonic Wars witnessed a boom in arcade construction across the continent and beyond. Between 1820 and 1840, at least a dozen arcades were built in Paris. Several others were opened beyond the French borders: in Milan, Bristol, Glasgow and Newcastle. The era also saw the architectural style exported beyond the borders of Europe, most notably to Philadelphia and Providence in America.

This second era of arcade construction was a period of invention and innovation. The Galerie Bordelaise in Bordeaux was the first arcade to cut through a block diagonally. In Liege, the Passage Lemonnier crossed two blocks of buildings. Opened in 1830, London's fashionable Lowther Arcade was constructed in the Greek revival style. Built in the form of a high corridor, divided into elegant bays, featuring a series of graceful internal arches and illuminated by tasteful rounded skylights, it was described as 'surpassing the Burlington Arcade in its architectural appearance.' New additions to the classic form also became fashionable, like the colonnade, the gallery and the glass dome. It was also a time when travel and travel writing made the architectural type better known throughout the world.

By the 1840s, the fashion for arcades, the ultimate symbol of civic and cultural modernity, was well-established.

1840-1860

During the decades of the mid-nineteenth century, the third era of arcade construction saw a move away from the spiritual homeland of the French capital. Parisian speculators increasingly turned to the new railway industry to turn a profit on their investments. Moreover, the reimagining of the city under the auspices of the legendary Baron Haussmann adopted a new focus: long avenues, broad boulevards, open spaces and public parks. Crucially, the period also saw pavements belatedly added to many Parisian streets. Despite the best efforts of Thomas Cook and Baedeker, allowing for large-scale tourism into the great city for the first time, the arcades of Paris were beginning to lose their lustre.

The highlights of this period are thus drawn from across the rest of the continent. Hamburg witnessed the construction of the gigantic Sillem's Bazaar, the first of several arcades built on German soil and for many years the largest in the world, a fact not lost on the city's proud residents. The citizens of the port city promenaded through this magnificently illuminated arcade in awe. Soon after, the stunning Galeries Saint-Hubert was opened in Brussels' old city. Having ceded from The Netherlands in 1830, Belgians saw the construction of the arcade as symbolic of the birth of a new, independent nation. This period was also noticeable for the fashion for arcades landing on distant shores, the Queens Arcade in Melbourne opening shortly after the middle of the century.

1860-1880

The following phase in the development of the arcade built upon the fashion for the great and the grand that characterised the previous era, taking it to the next level. The arcade which best illustrates the tastes of the third quarter of the nineteenth century is the monumental Galleria Vittorio Emanuele II in Milan. A cathedral to shopping, it was and remains the best-known arcade in the world.

The concept for the Galleria came from a series of public competitions aimed at encouraging suggestions for the development of the square in front of Il Duomo cathedral. Gradually, the idea for a public promenade between the cathedral and La Scala opera house took form. Eventually, the Bolognese architect Megnoni was granted the commission.

Megnoni's design took the form of a cross and incorporated a huge Roman triumphal arch. Topping the arcade was a dome, the diameter of which was exactly that of St Peter's in Rome. Richly decorated with frescos, the gallery also boasted statues of twenty-four famous Italians. More than any previous arcade, the construction of Galleria Vittorio Emanuele II represented an attempt to give a fresh focus to the centre of the city. It was to become the heart of the city.

Curiously, the Galleria was built by an English consortium, The City of Milan Improvement Company Ltd. The architect was assisted by a French engineer, making it a truly international endeavour. King Vittorio Emanuele II himself laid the foundation stone on 7th May 1865, though the triumphal arch was yet to be added. Tragically, the architect fell to his death from the arch during the completion process, which took over a decade.

The opening of the Galleria Vittorio Emanuele II launched both a fierce scramble to compete with its grandeur at home and an infectious craze to emulate its success abroad. Milan's jealous rivals were quick to follow in its footsteps, and the grand arcades in Turin, Genoa, Naples, Messina and Rome soon opened their doors. Moreover, in the four decades preceding the First World War, over one hundred Italian influenced arcades were built across Britain, including the renowned Burton Arcade in Manchester, a building modelled on the Milan arcade.

Surprisingly, though, the Italian effect was perhaps felt most strongly in ever-unfashionable Germany. The leaders of the new capital, Berlin, were keen to promote the city's self-image as the commercial and political heartland of the newly unified nation. This newfound enthusiasm was expressed in part through the construction of the Kaisergalerie, the arcade which introduced Berlin to the ranks of the .world's most fashionable cities.

The Kaisergalerie was Berlin's first modern commercial building. The arcade not only provided Berliners with some respite from the hectic Friedrichstrasse, but also offered a host of new amenities such as bars, restaurants, a concert hall, a hotel and a post office. The emperor himself conducted the opening ceremony in 1873, riding horseback through the arcade with his entourage to the delight of the adoring crowds – hence the name Kaisergalerie.

As in Italy, the lead taken by a single city was soon copied nationwide. In the following decades, more modest arcades appeared in the smaller German cities such as Frankfurt, Dresden, Cologne and Karlsruhe. However, like these and most other German arcades, the Kaisergalerie was destroyed in the Second World War.

1880-1900

The penultimate phase in the history of arcades coincided with an era when the fashion for the big and bold was taken to extremes. This era of the gigantic, typified by the building of both the Reichstag in Berlin and The Palace of Justice in Brussels, found its clearest and most vocal expression in the construction of the colossal Eiffel Tower in Paris, for many years the tallest structure on Earth.

This fashion for the gigantic was also mirrored in the design of arcades. Topping the list was the immense New Trade Halls in Moscow, the largest arcade complex built in the nineteenth century. Situated opposite the Kremlin in Red Square, and standing there to this day, this enormous complex of arcades replaced an entire district of residential and commercial buildings with a single colossal construction.

The New Trade Halls (known locally as GUM) consists of three parallel arcades, each of which extends some 250 metres. Criss-crossed by shorter connecting spaces, the arcades are far removed from the city's traffic and provide access to over one thousand shops. Built on three floors and interspersed with galleries, bridges and stairways, shopping in the New Trade Halls was an event in itself. Not to be outdone, city planners in the United States responded with the construction of the huge Cleveland Arcade, which boasts an incredible five levels of shops.

With the benefit of hindsight, it seems apparent that the construction of GUM and the Cleveland Arcade marked a turning point in the history of retailing, the fashion for the narrow, symmetrical, glass-roofed arcade slowly giving way to a trend for its more modern, less ornate, increasingly corporate counterpart – the shopping centre, or worse, the shopping mall.

1900-Date

Sometimes in history it is almost impossible to distinguish between the end of the beginning and the beginning of the end. The building of The Arcade in Dewsbury, however, most definitely falls into the latter category.

Around the turn of the twentieth century a number of factors coincided to call closing time on the relatively brief period of arcade construction across Europe and the wider world. Advancing medical knowledge stressed the need for fresh air and open spaces, dealing a further blow to the already dying trend of constructing buildings tightly closed in upon each other. Moreover, city planners were enthralled by the vogue for broad avenues and wide, open spaces, leaving arcades appearing outdated and out-of-place. New fire and building regulations made the construction of rows and terraces immeasurably more complex than building detached, stand-alone structures, especially in town and city centres. New types of building materials, especially concrete, were not suitable for the arcade architectural form. For arcades, the end was nigh!

Developments in wider society were significant too. By the late nineteenth century, the vast majority of the shopping public were low paid, most having little cash to spend on frivolities. They wanted cheap, mass-produced goods, and consequently arcades became increasingly seen as the preserve of the rich and privileged. Many arcades were given the prefix Royal, King's or Prince's in an attempt to conjure a sense of grandeur, though many shoppers were becoming increasingly unimpressed.

Some arcades attempted to enforce this air of exclusivity, employing a private security force, commonly known as the Beadles, to deter 'undesirables' and to maintain an atmosphere of contrived elegance. This was often the cause of conflict and regularly provoked a sense of injustice. One shopper was asked to leave The Corridor in Bath for wearing an apron and having his sleeves rolled up. Some arcades banned visitors from carrying parcels, opening umbrellas or singing. Even today, the Beadles at London's Burlington Arcade enforce a ban on whistling, running and 'acting boisterously' (only two people are not subject to the whistling ban, one is a schoolboy excused as a reward for a good school report, the other is Sir Paul McCartney!).

Most late nineteenth century/early twentieth century shoppers wanted proven quality, not luxury, a factor which was to work in the favour of the more modest arcades of provincial towns like Dewsbury. Most existing British arcades were built in that great period of urban expansion and modernisation in the half-century following 1860, the period from 1875 to 1900 being the most prolific. The architects of the regions were especially productive, the period seeing the building of seven arcades in Birmingham, five in Manchester, seven in Leeds and nine in Cardiff. The vast majority of these arcades, though architecturally faithful to the recognised form, were more functional and practical in purpose, a trend which ensured greater sustainability and longevity. Two exceptions, interestingly, were the Cross and County Arcades in Leeds, opened in 1901 and designed by the renowned Edwardian theatre architect Frank Matcham. Extravagant and theatrical, they were monuments to the wealth of the city and owed much to the Galleria Vittorio Emanuele II in Milan.

The post-Victorian era witnessed a marked reduction in the rate of arcade building. After 1910, those arcades that were built were mostly architecturally insignificant and mainly designed to a simple corridor plan. Usually constructed without façades, skylights or other adornments, they were often built in the cheapest possible manner.

Nearly every arcade ever built was constructed between the start of the French Revolution and the end of the First World War, a period of some 130 or so years. The people of late-Victorian Dewsbury were immensely fortunate to witness the construction of their own arcade in the penultimate decade of this era. Moreover, it's fascinating to think that, had it not been for the French Revolution, or for the filthy streets of late-eighteenth century Paris, The Arcade in Dewsbury may have never been built at all.

2

Grand Designs

Like many construction projects down the ages, the building of The Arcade in Dewsbury took longer than expected. Originally scheduled to open in 1897 to mark the long-reigning Queen's Diamond Jubilee, the building was due to be named 'The Victoria Arcade'. Given the unforeseen hold up and its eventual delayed opening in 1899 though, the simple title 'The Arcade' was thought more appropriate.

The Arcade was constructed according to designs by Albert Holmes Kirk of John Kirk & Sons, Huddersfield. Albert was the eldest of six children, three of whom followed in their father's footsteps to become architects in the family business. The Arcade was in some ways an exception that proved a rule, as the family focus was usually on the design and construction of chapels and churches, many of which stand to this day in and around the Huddersfield area. Other exceptions included a number of residential properties, a handful of mills and warehouses, two workhouses and Mirfield Town Hall. Young Albert must have visited lots of building sites and attended many an opening ceremony as a child and later as an apprentice architect.

Market Place in the early C20th. On the right, part of the sign for the Johnson & Balmford store is clearly visible. J&Bs would become a household name in the town. Below this, a young lad sells 'Cadamarteri's Famous Ices' from a two-wheeled cart, once a common and welcome sight in the area.

The building work, supervised by Mr Knowles, Chairman of the Dewsbury Board of Guardians, progressed over a series of separate stages. The late nineteenth-century buildings on Corporation Street were demolished first to make way for the northern entrance façade. The pre-existing buildings between Corporation Street through to Market Place were then gradually demolished to make way for the arcade, with the construction work proceeding in stages as demolition advanced southwards. The early nineteenth-century buildings on Market Place were due to be demolished last to create the southern entrance, though the current fabric of the building suggests that the plans were changed, and an earlier building was altered and retained. However, this building was fronted by the new façade, rendering this late revision invisible from street level.

The Arcade is approximately 62 metres long and narrows slightly towards the southern end. The building comprises a total of 26 units, one at either side of each of the two entrance archways and twenty-two inside. The façades at both ends are constructed from ashlar, a generic name for cut and dressed stone. Other building materials used throughout include coursed sandstone, red brick, Welsh slate, glass and cast-iron. Both internally and externally, the arcade to this day retains numerous authentic and early features, giving a true impression of its original appearance.

One of the best-known early C20th images of The Arcade. The subjects of the photo clearly failed to stand still for the cameraman, though this adds a certain quality to the image.

Though it might appear so at first glance, the northern and southern façades are not entirely identical, despite both consisting of three storeys plus an attic and Dutch gables. The carved lettering reading 'THE ARCADE' at the northern entrance incorporates a modest flower and shell motif, whereas the decoration above the similar lettering at the southern entrance is markedly more ornate. Also, the central window at the northern entrance has four sections, with three dividing mullions, and is embellished with a carved '1899' datestone, whereas the central window at the southern entrance has two sections, a single dividing mullion and little embellishment. Moreover, the southern façade is slightly narrower than the northern.

Internally the sandstone flagged-walkway is sheltered by an elegant cast-iron glazed roof with round-arched frames decorated with flowers and foliage. The timber shopfronts boast recessed doorways, some with integral display cases and many retaining tasteful tiling in a geometric pattern. Many of the moulded door and window architraves are originals, as are some of the stairs, panelled doors, built-in cupboards and cast-iron fireplaces. One of the shops sports a first-floor trapdoor with a hoist winch beam above, which was at one time used to haul musical instruments up from the ground floor for repair. The upper floors of the southern entrance block retain original cornicing, chimney breasts, balustrades and stained-glass oriel windows.

The overall impression is of a building displaying a restrained Renaissance style with subtle detailing and a quality finish. It is a good example of a late nineteenth-century arcade that is faithful to the tradition first imported from Europe almost a century earlier.

3

🙠

Early Opening

In the late nineteenth century, many successful entrepreneurs came to Dewsbury to seek their fortune and to open up businesses. Many made a huge impact on the town's retail trade, making good profits, living in fine houses and employing servants. Luckily, some had the foresight to recognise the opportunities that were presented by the opening of The Arcade in 1899.

Three shops were demolished to make way for the southern, Market Place entrance to The Arcade. The first was Hampshire's Exchange and Mart, which was described as a 'Smallware and Hardware Merchant'. The second, 'S. Dawson and Son, Lithographers, Printers and Stationers', subsequently took up residence in the unit at the left-hand side of the northern, Commercial Street entrance to the newly-opened The Arcade. The third was William Ballance's Flowers, Fruit and Seeds shop.

Ballance had previously had a shop at the bottom end of Wakefield Road. The building had been demolished around fifteen years earlier, however, to make way for the construction of the new Town Hall, which was opened in 1889, a decade earlier than The Arcade. As compensation for the demolition of his business premises, it appears that Ballance was offered the shop at Number 27 Market Place by way of consolation. Despite also having this second shop demolished to make way for a grander building, Ballance refused to be defeated, taking up residence in the unit on the right-hand side of the southern entrance to The Arcade (at more or less the same location), where he remained for many years.

Three shops were demolished to make way for the Market Place entrance façade. They were Hampshire's Exchange and Mart, Dawson's Lithographers, Printers and Stationers and Ballance's Flowers, Fruit and Seeds.

Ballance was a respected member of the town's business community. In long black coat and sporting a bowler hat, he cut an impressive figure. He lived at one time in a grand house at the crest of Leeds Road. This later became a pub, The Whistler, and later still, Tesco. As a devotee of Dewsbury Rugby League Club, the residence was conveniently located close to his beloved Crown Flatt.

Another well-known local businessman was the prolific Marsden Oates. Trading in knitting wool and knitted garments, Oates had six shops throughout the area, including three in Dewsbury. He was helped in the business by two of his sons, John and George, with whom he and the rest of the family lived in a large Victorian house on Eightlands Road.

Oates was never afraid to take a risk, and when the new arcade opened in town, he was one of the first to move in, taking the second unit up on the right, next to Ballance's. He was quick to utilise the upstairs rooms, where twelve women made knitted garments for sale in the shop downstairs. The arcade shop was a thriving concern in the opening decade of the twentieth century.

Following the outbreak of the First World War, however, four of Oates' five sons had to take up arms. Lacking sufficient staff, and with labour in short supply as the country was set upon a war footing, he was forced to close most of his shops. The shop in The Arcade, however, remained open until 1956, when it finally succumbed to fierce competition and the arrival of synthetic fibres.

Still prominent on the town's skyline, the Oates family home was a large, stone-built, double-fronted house with a long driveway leading to stables. With a large private garden and overlooking the train station, the Oates residence also became a pub in later life – the Eightlands Well.

John Oates, centre, and his brother George, right, helped their father Marsden Oates run the family wool and woollen garments business. On the left in the bowler hat is William Ballance, who ran the florists next door.

Another recognised figure in the local retail community was John Jubb, who was described as a 'clothier'. Jubb's Tailors was quick to take up position on the left-hand side of the Market Place entrance to the arcade, opposite Ballance's Florist. Jubb's were famed for their straw hats, which were sold at sixpence ha'penny each or three for one shilling and sixpence. As was made clear by the 'Also at the Top End' window display, the business also had a shop at the Corporation Street entrance to the arcade (on the same side, and therefore at the right-hand side of the northern entrance).

Jubb's was also affected by the events of the Great War.

Before joining the King's Own Yorkshire Light Infantry, John Carlton Kendall had been an assistant in the Jubb's shop at the 'top end' of the arcade. In the spring of 1917, he saw significant action in France, receiving a critical wound to the chest and left arm, which had to be amputated. He died at No.11 Stationery Hospital on 15th May 1917, aged just 24, and is buried at St Sever Cemetery, Rouen.

Taken from inside The Arcade, this photo shows a very well-stocked side window at Jubb's. As indicated at the foot of the window display, Jubb's were 'Also at the Top End', having a store at the northern entrance of the same side of The Arcade.

Just over a year later tragedy struck the business for a second time. Luther Roebuck had been the manager of the same Corporation Street shop before joining up with The Royal Field Artillery in March of 1917. Three months later he was deployed overseas and was soon on the front line. On 13th August he suffered a serious shrapnel wound to the head, sustained in action around Nieuwpoort in Belgium. After receiving hospital treatment, at first abroad and later in Keighley, he was finally discharged in December 1917. Although in ill-health, he returned to Jubb's in the early part of the following year, eventually succumbing to his injuries on 10th June 1918, aged just 31. John Jubb acted as one of the coffin bearers at his funeral at Dewsbury Cemetery, where his gravestone can still be seen.

In the following decade Jubb's became part of the neighbouring Johnson and Balmford business, and the oft-photographed first-floor 'Jubb's' sign that adorned Number 23 Market Place for many years was replaced by the equally recognisable 'J&Bs' lettering.

Market Day, Market Place, Dewsbury

The southern façade in the inter-war years, perhaps the late 1920s. Jubb's Tailors has been taken over by Johnson & Balmford and is now a 'J&BS Cash Store'. Ballance's Florists is still a thriving concern.

The next shop up on the left from Jubb's Market Place outlet was D. Douglas Shoe Shop, established by David and Julia Douglas at the turn of the twentieth century and one of the first businesses to open in the arcade. The shop was spread over three units, and was a popular choice for quality, no-nonsense footwear. Later the business would pass into the hands of three of David and Julia's children: Mary, James and Ellen Douglas. Mary later married a local musician, Charles Auty, with whom she established a music shop at the opposite side of the arcade – the celebrated 'C.T. Auty - The Music Shop'. Later still, the shoe shop would pass into the hands of the renowned Ivor Burns, though the business continued be known formally as 'D. Douglas' and maintained a registered office in the arcade until its eventual closure in the early part of this century. The D. Douglas name thus graced the arcade for over a century. The sign for the registered office remains on the door of the vacant unit to this day.

The first four decades of the twentieth century were good times for the retailers of the arcade, and most businesses made good profits. Many of the shops became household names within the town and were recognised for the quality and value of their products. Businesses came and went, as they always do, but the arcade as a whole remained a thriving, bustling, profitable concern. It wasn't all plain sailing, though.

The longstanding issues with the landlords and custodians of the arcade were apparent from the very beginning. At first, none of the shops in the arcade had toilets or running water. There was a first-floor toilet at the top of some steps part way down the arcade, but this was a public toilet. Because of the lack of water supply, the proprietors understandably thought that they ought not to have to pay water rates. Moreover, as the toilet was a public toilet, the shopkeepers further suggested that this facility should not count against the water rates. The water authority, however, argued that as the arcade had a glazed roof from which rainwater was dispersed into the drains, and that this was part of the wider water management system, this justified the charging of water rates. The proprietors were left with no choice but to pay (the glass roof was a cause for complaint throughout the entire history of the arcade, and indeed has been an ongoing and familiar concern for most arcade owners and landlords).

One of the many postcards of The Arcade produced in the early years of the C20th.

Many other famous names in the history of retailing in Dewsbury were made in the arcade. Although perhaps not established at the very beginning, some took up residence in the early days and were to go on to become highly regarded by the townsfolk.

Designed by Albert Holmes Kirk of Huddersfield, The Arcade opened in 1899, a time when horse drawn carriages were still a common sight on the streets of Dewsbury.

In the early 1920s, J&B's had taken over the 'bottom end' shop formerly occupied by Jubb's, a few years before the better-known department store on 'busy corner', which could also be accessed via the arcade, was established in 1926. Prior to hosting C.T. Auty, the units opposite D. Douglas Shoe Shop were occupied by a popular predecessor, F. Normington, who first used the uncomplicated suffix 'The Music Shop'. The much-loved fancy goods outlet, Forrest's, known for its fine perfumes and superior accessories, was established as a shoppers' favourite long before the Second World War. Purveyors of quality leather goods, Walco, set up shop in the arcade in 1937, and were to provide leather satchels to the town's schoolchildren for many decades to come.

The arcade decorated with bunting to mark the Coronation of King George V in 1911. On the left, illuminated globes light the way into the D. Douglas Shoe Shop.

The pre-war years were in many ways the golden years for The Arcade. The town centre was almost always busy, and the arcade was something of a focal point. Decorated with bunting, flowers and Union Jacks, the familiar photos of public events, such as the coronation of King George V in 1911, show the arcade at its best. The post-war years, however, offer a history that is richer still – living memories.

The first two shops to take up position at either side of
the Market Place entrance to the arcade were John Jubb's
Tailors and Ballance's Flowers, Fruit and Seeds. The new
Ballance's store occupied more or less the same location
as the previous shop, demolished to make way for the
southern façade.

Part Two
In Living Memory

4

&

C.T. Auty 'The Music Shop'

Memories of C.T. Auty 'The Music Shop' – 1949 to the mid-1970s
by Josephine Ripley (nee Auty)

My family's association with the arcade goes all the way back to the grand opening in 1899 when my maternal grandfather and grandmother, David and Julia Douglas, opened one of the very first shops. It was on the opposite side of the arcade to where my mum and dad would later open Auty's Music Shop and was called 'D. Douglas Shoe Shop'. It was quite a big shop, taking up three units. One unit sold ladies' shoes, one unit sold men's shoes, and the other unit was a more general, mixed unit. The shop occupied the site for generations and remained open long after the establishment of Auty's. I remember that, in the shop's later years, they seemed to sell very old-fashioned fitting shoes. When I think back, the ladies who bought them all appeared very old, but they were probably younger than I am now, and you wouldn't see me wearing those shoes!

Eventually, ownership of the shoe shop passed to the next generation, with three siblings all becoming shareholders. They were: my mother Mary Auty (nee Douglas), my aunt Ellen Winterbottom (nee Douglas) and my uncle James Douglas (a family legend says that James walked up the arcade, unaided, at the age of 9 months!). It was a very successful shop, so much so that they often stayed open until 10pm on a Saturday night. Eventually, much later, it became Ivor Burns shoe shop.

Charles Thomas Auty, known universally as Tom. Along with wife Mary, Tom established C.T. Auty 'The Music Shop' in 1949. Mary Auty (nee Douglas) was the daughter of David and Julia Douglas, founders of D. Douglas Shoe Shop. Mary had been granted shares in the footwear business by her parents, though she sold them to fund the founding of Auty's.

My dad was a professional drummer and had his own dance band. He also played in the orchestra pit in Dewsbury's famous Empire Theatre, which was just opposite the Town Hall, on the site where Empire House now stands. He also played regularly at the Marmaville Club in Mirfield. In the late 1940s, though, my mum and dad decided to open a music shop. My mum took her shares out of the shoe shop, my dad sold his drum kit, and C.T. Auty's Music Shop was born, opening in 1949, exactly fifty years after the opening of my grandparents' shoe shop (the C.T. stands for Charles Thomas, though everyone knew my dad as Tom). I believe that a music shop called F. Normington's had occupied the site prior to my mum and dad taking over, as I remember seeing the name stamped on the sheet music, but I'm not entirely sure.

I was only two years old when Mum and Dad went in together to establish Auty's. One of my earliest memories is of Mum dropping me off at the nursery in Thornhill Lees. I would stand at the window and watch as she walked away – on her way to work in the new shop. She would ring the nursery as soon as she arrived at work, but I was always absolutely fine by then and occupied with something else.

In 1962, at the age of 15, I joined my mum and dad and went to work in the shop. I remember the next few years very well. It was a really busy time, as it was at the dawn of Beatlemania. I remember seeing huge stacks of Beatles singles being carried down the arcade for delivery.

The shop was a veritable Aladdin's Cave in those days. It sold drums, guitars (both acoustic and electric), trumpets, cornets, clarinets, flutes and penny whistles (though we used the proper name for penny whistles – flageolets). It also sold more modest instruments like harmonicas, jaw harps, recorders and kazoos, as well as all kinds of musical related toys. We also sold an instrument called the autoharp. These are a bit like a zither, although slightly different in that they have a series of bars designed to mute the strings - other than those needed for the chord that you are trying to play. I don't think we sold too many of those. My dad did instrument repairs in one of the rooms upstairs, so we had that side to the business too.

We had lots of interesting customers in those days and saw a few famous faces over the years. Labi Siffre came in one time to buy some manuscript paper. He must have been writing music at the time, so I hope he composed one of his best songs on that paper! A regular visitor was local favourite Sammy King, of Sammy King and The Voltaires fame. Sammy is best known for writing Penny Arcade, which was a huge worldwide hit for Roy Orbison in 1969. Sammy and the band used to come in for guitar strings and the like, which they would otherwise have had to go to Leeds to buy. In fact, quite a lot of musicians that were performing at Batley Variety Club would pop in for essentials, like saxophone reeds etc (Here's an interesting post-script. One of the top local musical agents and promoters of that era was a man called Bernard Hinchcliffe. Bernard couldn't swim at the time, though later in life he decided to learn. Coincidentally, I had become a swimming teacher by then, and I was the one to give him private lessons. Upon learning to swim, he played a trick on his wife by throwing himself into a pool in Spain and pretending to drown. Luckily, he had become well trained to swim to safety – thanks to me!).

We had our regular customers too, though. I remember one particular chap called Lesley Boot. He was a painter and decorator by day, but at night he was Dewsbury's top country and western fan. He would browse all the catalogues and buy just about every country album on release. There was something of a pattern in our other regulars' visits. On Saturdays the place was heaving with kids buying records and cassette tapes etc but on weekdays it was more often music teachers who would come in to buy sheet music for specific pieces that they were teaching in their piano lessons.

The arcade was thriving during my time there and had lots of great shops. J&B's Department Store was always very busy and had a lovely upstairs toy department. Nearby was Forrest's, a fancy goods shop which was great for perfumes, cosmetics and handbags etc. Then there was Walco leather goods, which sold wallets, purses and school satchels. I can still smell Walco's right now! Next to us was a tiny tobacconist, which seemed not much more than a hole in the wall. I remember that the proprietor was called Miss Lodge at one time. Further down was the sweet shop, which was filled with jars of lovely old-fashioned sweets. Then there was Christine's Florists, which was very popular. My mum's family's shoe shop was still there for much of that time too, and I often used to pop over at lunchtimes for a natter. One particular favourite, though, was Ann's Pantry. They sold the best Eccles Cakes I've ever tasted! You had to pop to Ann's in the morning if you wanted to buy an Eccles Cake because if you went in the afternoon, they would all be gone!

One unpleasant memory from that era is of the break-in. A number of burglars entered by removing some of the slate tiles, having climbed up and over the roof from Foundry Street. They weren't the brightest sparks, though, as they only took a guitar. Most of the objects of significant value would have been too heavy for them to escape with and carry back down the same way they had come in. They left a heck of a mess behind though!

My mum, dad and I worked together in the shop for many years. Eventually, though, circumstances began to change, as they always do. The shop came under increasing competition, especially when WHSmiths opened. They seemed to take all the cream as far as sales of the Top 10 singles went, though luckily we had other products and services which set us apart and sustained the business. Then, sadly, my dad died, at the age of 65. He had been a heavy smoker. Having a shop next to a tobacconist, from where he bought his favourite Gold Flake cigarettes, probably didn't help. My mum was getting older too and wasn't in the best of health.

Eventually, I got married and went to live in Kirkheaton. My daughter, Sally, was a winter baby, born in December.

In the new year I remember having to take her to the shop, where she stayed with me all day. My mum wasn't well enough to work full-time, so she would come down at lunchtimes, which were always busy, to help out. One of the abiding memories of that time is of hearing my mum walking up the arcade, as I could hear her heels click-clicking as she approached.

Finally, and after the best part of three decades, we decided to close the business. The rates in the arcade were becoming ridiculous, and the shop was no longer profitable. My husband had a motor business, so I decided to go and work with him. It was more money, plus I could work from home. Two local businessmen took over the lease, and the shop continued to trade as a music shop.

It's heart-warming to know that so many people have fond memories of Auty's Music Shop and makes me feel very proud. The shop has been closed for many years now, but luckily the name lives on through my nephew Peter Auty. Peter became head choir boy at St Paul's Cathedral and sang at Charles and Diana's wedding in 1981. He also sang on the original recording of 'Walking in the Air' from the soundtrack of the Christmas movie 'The Snowman'. This was before Aled Jones recorded his version of the song. Peter remains a professional operatic tenor and has worked with most of the major British opera companies and a number of companies across Europe too. The proud musical tradition within the Auty family thus continues to thrive and will hopefully do so for decades to come!

Memories of Auty's Music Shop – Mid 1970s to 1997
by Gerald Pearson

I come from a very musical family. My grandfather, John William Pearson, sang with Huddersfield Choral Society for many years. Following in his footsteps, my dad also became a musician, learning his trade in the pre-war years. Later, he played in an orchestra which performed at Saturday night dances in and around the Dewsbury area, including at the Town Hall. The act was called 'George Pearson and his Embassy Orchestra' and was very active in the 1940s and 50s. Prior to this he had been in the Spen Valley Accordion Band. I myself was in several rock bands in the 1960s, the most successful being 'The Sinfonics'. We played all the pubs, clubs and dancehalls in and around West Yorkshire, as well as at Batley Town Hall and, like my father before me, at Dewsbury Town Hall. Moreover, my grandson Jonathan Pearson is a classical guitarist and has played at the Youth Proms at the Royal Albert Hall as a member of Calderdale Guitar Ensemble. My wife and I toured Western Australia with the ensemble a number of years ago, to watch them perform and to act as guardians for the 18 strong group. My daughter Sharon is an accomplished flautist and our other two grandchildren, Jessica and Cherie, are very good light opera singers.

My family's association with Auty's Music Shop began when, in the mid-1970s, the shop was purchased from the Auty family by my brother Keith Pearson and his business partner Bill Price. Keith was a well-known folk musician, playing fiddle not only in The Tykes Ceilidh Band but also for the Spen Valley Longsword Team. Bill on the other hand was an accomplished folk singer, with several LP records to his name.

When Bill and Keith took over the lease of The Music Shop from the Auty family it had previously been managed by Josephine, who I believe was the daughter of Charles Auty. They decided to stick with the name as the business was a limited company listed under that name and also had a bank account in the name, so it would have been a lot of effort to change to a new one. Plus, the shop had a great reputation and was trusted for its high standards amongst the townsfolk, which counts for a lot. So, the name lived on!

The business was situated in 12-14 The Arcade and had two retail spaces downstairs and three rooms upstairs. One upstairs room was used as an office, one had some booths for listening to records and the third was a utility room where Mr Auty had previously done instrument repairs etc (the main sales room of the shop had a trap door in the ceiling through which Mr Auty would haul big instruments up to the first floor by block and tackle).

One early problem that the partners encountered was that Bill was unable to give enough time to the business. Bill was quite a well-known musician and would occasionally tour across Canada. He was a director of the business, but his main interests were in singing and in playing the guitar, which were his passions. I was working full-time at that time but would also often deputise for Bill by working in the shop on Saturdays when he was on tour. Eventually, Keith suggested that I take over from Bill as a partner in the business. As a result, in November 1978, I bought Bill's share in the business. Bill was quite happy to be relieved of his duties, I suspect, and was quite content to continue to pursue his musical ambitions.

We two brothers together ran the shop successfully for many years. Record sales were a very important aspect of our business model. We had accounts with all the major record companies, from whom we bought direct. We always took great pride in being able to get any record, however rare, for even the most discerning customer. We used a catalogue called Music Master, which came in two volumes, to order anything we didn't have in stock. Later, we sold cassettes and, later still, CDs. Other aspects were important too, though. We had contracts with schools for the supply of recorders and recorder books. We also provided sheet music for piano teachers, who would often come in looking for specific pieces for lessons. Guitar sales were also profitable, especially at Christmas. We sold Yamaha and Casio keyboards as well. Sometimes, people would buy keyboards from Argos, but they would come to us for advice on how to play and operate them. Also, were always local musicians' first port of call for accessories like reeds, strings and plectrums.

We provided a number of services too, including guitar lessons, which were held in one of the upstairs rooms every Saturday and which were quite successful for a while. I ran a short course for beginners, focusing on the basics like a few simple chords and strumming styles etc. The course consisted of six 45-minute lessons. We also had a colleague called Colin who taught classical guitar. Sometimes, though, I suspected that parents brought their kids for guitar lessons just so they could do their shopping in peace for a while! Furthermore, my brother and I both did instrument repairs. I repaired guitars and Keith repaired violins, including restringing bows. There were some unique aspects to the business, too. I was employed as an industrial chemist, working with dyes. I used my knowledge to make and colour tassels for majorettes' maces and batons. We also sold some unusual instruments, like the bell lyre, which is a bit like a hand-held glockenspiel and is used by marching bands.

The shop was a real family business. My son and daughter both worked in the shop on Saturdays at one time. It was during the era of coloured disk and picture disk singles, and I used to let them both choose one as part of their wages (I kept some of these special disks until, quite recently, I sold them for a fair bit of cash!). The job was a bit of extra money for the kids too. I worked full-time in the chemical industry but would always take the week before Christmas as one of my holidays, to give them a hand in the shop during the busiest week of the year (we ran a Christmas club, where customers could make regular payments over the course of the year to build up credits towards festive purchases. As a result, Christmas Eve was always absolute chaos, and we would often sell out of certain items). Moreover, if Keith took a week's holiday during the summer to attend Whitby Folk Festival, I would take a week's holiday at the same time so that I could deputise for him in the shop.

The arcade was very busy during most of our time there. It was on the route between the bus station and the market, and everybody saw the arcade as the main thoroughfare between the two. There was a lovely atmosphere in the arcade, too. It was a great community, and everyone used to look out for each other. Anyone who worked in the arcade could get a discount in all the other shops, which was always useful. We used to place speakers outside the shop to play a bit of background music for the shoppers and to create a nice ambience. There were some great shops in the arcade as well. One particular favourite was J&B's. I remember, in earlier times, every Christmas Santa would arrive outside J&B's on a fire engine. Then he would climb up a ladder and clamber through the first-floor window into the toy department, where his grotto was ready and waiting for him. Auty's was quite nice too, though, I should add. I remember at one time there being a decorative piece of glass across the top of the window with the traditional 'His Master's Voice' dog and gramophone player emblem showing. I bet that would be worth a lot of money now!

Throughout my time as proprietor of the shop I often encountered reminders of the earlier era of the Auty family's reign. On one occasion, when searching through the middle room upstairs, we discovered literally thousands of pieces of old sheet music, ranging from a full orchestral score for a symphony orchestra to single sheets of pop music from the time. It was all stored in racks which, had they been placed in a single stack, would probably have measured over 20 feet in height! Rather than destroy all this sheet music we decided to do a special promotion and sold it all at the original prices of sixpence or a shilling etc. The Dewsbury Reporter ran an accompanying article in the newspaper at the time and we had people coming from all over to browse through the racks, some even spending a whole afternoon browsing for hours in the upstairs room.

In the 1940's and 50's The Music Shop didn't just sell everything musical but also looked to sell more or less anything that would turn a profit. Not long after the family took over the lease, we discovered that the third upstairs room contained an incredibly diverse range of leftover items. Who remembers John Bull Printing Sets, Meccano and Bayko Building Sets? If you remember them fondly, you would have had a field day! There were also about half a dozen busts of Winston Churchill and a couple of small Tan-Sad child's tricycles - the type with the pedals attached to the front wheel. I sold the tricycles recently for a tidy profit. I didn't mind going upstairs, as every time I went up there, I would find something new. My daughter, Sharon, however, was convinced that the upstairs rooms were haunted and would always avoid going up there if possible. Keith, however, did his best to play on this and would always be thinking of reasons to send her up!

On another occasion, when we decided to decorate the stairway to the upstairs rooms, we discovered a cupboard in the office which had clearly been painted over many times. When it was finally opened, we were amazed to find literally hundreds of paintings contained within. The whole range included a few oil paintings, some small water colours, several prints of works by well-known artists and a number of ink drawings. Many years ago, I had a couple of the paintings valued at The Antiques Roadshow. One of the paintings, a landscape depicting a river rolling through the Derbyshire countryside, painted in 1895, was valued at £1000! It must be worth a bit more by now. Many of the paintings were water damaged, but some are still in good condition. It's still a problem of what to do with them all!

One of our discoveries had a royal connection. In the summer of 1953, the arcade was decorated with bunting along its full length to commemorate the coronation of Queen Elizabeth II. This bunting was also discovered hidden in The Music Shop. I used it later for street parties etc and it is still in my possession. If it is of any use in the future, I'd be glad to see it restored to its original home in the arcade.

I recall a time when Dewsbury featured quite regularly in various TV programmes, usually period dramas which required 'old style' authentic settings. Local locations used included the court in Dewsbury Town Hall and the old Dewsbury Hospital. The Arcade itself once featured in an episode of Heartbeat, a feelgood police drama set in 1960s North Yorkshire. The episode in question was entitled 'Bringing it all Back Home' and featured Nick Berry, Bill Maynard (as the legendary loveable rogue, Greengrass) and the famous Freddie Davies, who starred as the owner of a seaside arcade which sported several penny slot machines.

The story was centred around a typical Greengrass ruse where his dog would sit by a slot machine and wag its tail, signifying for Greengrass to play and win. The filming took place inside No.10, as this unit was empty at the time. The TV Company brought in some old slot machines to make the place look authentic. Auty's Music Shop was right next door to No.10. Consequently, we were asked to hang seaside items for sale outside the shop to disguise the pop posters and other music memorabilia that wouldn't have been around at the time. We had beachballs, buckets and spades and hula hoops displayed on the outside of the shop for the benefit of the shots taken looking down the arcade. They also parked an old bus at the bottom entrance to the arcade to block the view of Yorkshire Bank and the ATM cash dispensers, which obviously wouldn't have been around at that time. The whole time for filming took over 5 hours for a shown clip of around a couple of minutes.

Towards the end of our time in the arcade the business became increasingly unprofitable, in every sense of the word. Rates were around £12,000 per annum at one stage, making generating a decent income very difficult. The management company would often be chasing us for the money and weren't always particularly understanding. They weren't especially responsive to our needs, either. They were terrible at repairs and at maintaining the roof and the drainage system wasn't fit for purpose. We had a fractured downpipe running down the steps which sometimes leaked and the roof gullies would often overflow and rainwater would run down the walls and into the shop. We also had a break in on one occasion. Someone climbed up and over the roof from the yard where the side entrance to Woolworths used to be. Whoever it was, they only took a guitar, though they damaged lots of the roof tiles in the process.

The doors of 'The Music Shop' were open for well over a century. Though the shop traded under a number of different proprietors, the provision of quality musical instruments, a vast catalogue of recordings and a wide range of related equipment was a constant.

Unfortunately, in 1996, by brother Keith died. My wife, the children and I ran the shop for a further six months or so, but we were unable to give it our full attention due to other commitments. Eventually, we sold the business to Steve Lister in 1997. He moved the business across the arcade to Number 15.

Steve became a good friend, and we were happy to support him. Like with my brother before him, if Steve went on holiday for a week, I would cover for him in the shop. In fact, he would often go to our holiday home in Wales. On one occasion we bought a flute from Steve, finally, after all those years, becoming customers of the shop. But it was all to no avail. After 2 or 3 years, Steve sold the business to a music shop in Huddersfield which soon after closed the shop for good.

My wife and I are very proud to have run Auty's Music Shop for all those years. Music is our love, and they were the best and happiest times of our lives. We met some of the most interesting people from all over the country. It was heart-breaking to watch the arcade fall into disrepair and to eventually close. I'm so glad that steps are being taken to re-open the arcade and it's a great pleasure to be a small part of it.

Memories of Auty's Music Shop – 2005 to 2009
by Maureen Crawshaw

My ex-husband and I bought Auty's Music Shop from
Steve Lister in February of 2005. Steve had taken over
the business from the previous proprietors a few years
earlier, at which point he had moved the shop to No.15,
a small unit at the opposite side of the arcade from its
best remembered location at Nos. 12-14. We bought the
business lock, stock and barrel, including all the fixtures,
fittings and a Panasonic Music System. We decided not
to change the name of the business, as the shop had a
longstanding good reputation in the town.

Having established GTR Guitars in Huddersfield's
Byram Arcade in 1999, we had been in the retail trade
for a few years by the time we bought Auty's. We had
a number of instrument shops in Byram Arcade at
different times during the early 2000s. As well as GTR,
which was focused mainly on electric guitars, we also
had a shop that specialised in acoustic guitars and
another that sold drums and basses. We also had a shop
on Wood Street for a few years. We then became aware
of the opportunity to branch out into Dewsbury and
decided to take the plunge.

It's fair to say that our shop in The Arcade was more of a
strictly modern musician's outlet than its predecessors.
Our main focus was electric guitars, keyboards,
songbooks, effects pedals, strings, cables, amplifiers etc.
There wasn't much demand for sheet music for classical
piano at the time. We also stocked CDs and did good

business in selling a range of 'best of' and 'greatest hits' compilations from racks outside the shop.

There was a lovely atmosphere along the arcade at that time and some really nice people worked there. It was still quite a busy place, especially on Wednesday and Saturday mornings, when the market would draw the shoppers out bright and early. I always found it strange how the town was quiet by mid-afternoon on market days, the crowds having picked off all the best bargains hours earlier. There were some great shops in the arcade too. There was a sweet shop, a comic shop, a socks and underwear shop, a lovely café and of course Ivor Burns shoe shop. There were some great places for lunch nearby, too – like Val's Coffee Shop.

Despite the pleasant working environment, things became increasingly difficult for the business over the short period of our tenure at The Arcade. Dewsbury suffered terribly from the closure of Marks & Spencer in 2007, after which there was a marked downturn in trade. It seemed that people just didn't want to visit the town anymore. The owners of the arcade didn't make things easier, either. The stairs up to the toilet weren't fit for purpose and the roof leaked. We had buckets out in the arcade to catch the rainwater, which doesn't exactly attract customers. The owners didn't do anything, though, and were never to be seen.

The business was becoming less and less profitable, too. You can't turn a profit by selling a couple of packets of guitar strings every day. To make things worse, we had a number of shoplifting incidents. On one occasion, a guy just walked in, grabbed a guitar and walked straight back out with it, bold as brass, and without even attempting to conceal his crime.

Eventually, and with a deep sense of regret, we decided to close the shop (I believe it was in 2009). I was devastated to have to put up the closed sign on such a historic music shop and it was a low point in a very distressing period. I was so upset that I paid for an announcement in the Dewsbury Reporter to mark the closure. We left with over a year to run on the lease, which we continued to pay until the lease came to an end. The whole process was nothing short of traumatic. I couldn't bring myself to visit the town for years. When I finally plucked up the courage, the arcade had closed and all I could do was take a photo of the arcade through the closed shutters. It was so sad!

Anyway, as that's all water under the bridge, I'll sign off on a happier note. Although I worked in the Auty's shop myself at times, the Dewsbury arm of the business was mainly managed by my son, Martin Chung. I proud to say that Martin kept the musical tradition of Auty's Music Shop very much alive and continues to do so to this day. Better known as Chungy, he is a professional musician and plays in the 'Invaders of the Heart', the backing band of the legendary Jah Wobble, touring the UK and overseas on a regular basis and occasionally performing at festivals. Moreover, in a remarkable coincidence, in his other band - 'Big Wave' - he performed in Dewsbury Market Place at The Arcade Group's 'Summer Gathering' in August of 2021. Perhaps he'll perform at The Arcade's reopening ceremony in a couple of years' time.

What they said about Auty's Music Shop

I bought my first record from Auty's in the arcade. It was 'Not Fade Away' by The Rolling Stones. – Janet Holmes

Auty's was a shop that sold musical instruments and was half-way down on the left. I bought my first mouth organ there and it had drums, guitars, mandolins and saxophones displayed in the window. I loved going in and looking around. – Mike Mann

I bought my first two single records there – in 1962! You could buy three singles for a pound. They sold sheet music too. – Geoff Hardwick

Auty's was great. They used to have a small but very eccentric selection of albums: Cilla Black, James Last, John Denver and Black Sabbath!! – Michael Pickles

I worked in Auty's Music Shop in 1961. Mr Auty was a good boss. It was a really great arcade! – Sylvia Kellett

Auty's Music Shop also sold drum major majorette maces. As a child in the 1980s I used to dream of owning one as I gazed lustfully at them through the shop window. Then my grandma, Eileen Wilkinson (who was the lollipop lady at Thornhill High School), came into a little cash and bought me one for a very special Christmas present. I loved my mace and used to practice for hours. I practiced every day for years. I used to be quite a twirler back in the day! – Michelle Wilkinson

My son started guitar lessons at Auty's in the 1990s. It was about 75p for a half an hour lesson. I just had time to nip into the Black Bull for a swift half! – Sheila Higgins

I remember a music shop called Auty's. I would buy my records there. I would also ask for any used or unwanted band posters that had been used for record promotions so that I could make a music-based wallpaper for my bedroom as a child and teenager. They were always given free of charge. – Alison Ozbey

I bought my first guitar from Auty's Music Shop! – Tony Jackson

I remember going to Auty's music shop in the Arcade. It was very good for buying sheet music for my piano lessons at that time and the staff were always very helpful. – Keith Webster

I remember visiting Auty's Music Shop at the age of six to get my first musical instrument - a recorder! I remember passing a man with an eye patch who stood outside at the top of the arcade - selling jumping beans! All great 1970s and 1980s memories. – P Jackson

When my son was learning keyboard and guitar, we bought lots of books from Auty's. – Jennifer Graham

Auty's was fantastic for ordering obscure, independently released 'punk' or 'new wave' singles that we would read about in NME or Sounds and would otherwise have to go to Leeds or Wakefield to find. The owner would order them for us without judgement. Sometimes he would have a selection in, and we would browse the records amongst the violins and saxophones on the walls. – Mark Martin

Auty's was where we bought all my son's music when he was learning to play the piano. – Jean Reece

'From Me to You' by The Beatles was just one of the many records I bought at Auty's in The Arcade, and you always got the free outer sleeve. – Stewart Bunting

Auty's Music Shop was where my mum bought me the Premier snare drum on which I learned music. Even when I had different kits and was having a great time playing in bands, I still kept my snare separate. – Andrew Smith

In 1960 I used to look in Auty's window and stare at a white 'Lucky 7' guitar. It was £13, which was like 6 weeks' wages then. I saved forever to buy it. – George Jenkinson

Fantastic arcade and fantastic shop! Very sad fact that this icon of Dewsbury has closed! – Dave Smith

He introduced me to Fender Super Bullets (electric guitar strings with a .008 top e string). Never looked back! Got my music books there too. If he hadn't got it, he ordered it! Sorely missed! – Gary Armitage

My ex said that he used to play guitar in a band, so I thought I would surprise him by buying a gorgeous electric guitar and amplifier from Auty's for him – and it wasn't cheap! I even hid it at my sister's house until his birthday. Well, what would you know? The look on his face when I gave to him it was not surprise, but sheer shock, as he couldn't play a bloody note. Lying toad! – Sherrel Oldroyd

5

℘

Beaumont and Blackburn Electricals

Memories of Beaumont and Blackburn Electricals
by David Blackburn

My family holds a very special honour in the history of retailing in Dewsbury. My father was the first ever customer to shop in the Dewsbury branch of Marks & Spencer, which opened in 1908. My grandfather was the manager of Freeman, Hardy and Willis's shoe shop, which was just across the road from the soon to open M&S, (the chosen location for the new shop was on Westgate, in the premises which was later occupied by J.W. Thornes Electricals). The family lived over the shoe shop and eagerly observed the preparations for the big day. My grandfather promised my father that when M&S opened, he would take him across and buy him a present. My grandfather told my father that he could choose anything that he wanted, which wasn't as generous as it sounds, as everything in the famous 'Penny Bazaar' cost a penny. Sure enough, as soon as the shutters opened, my father was in like a shot. He

65

bought a monkey on a stick, a suitable gift for a four-year old. Many decades later, at the age of seventy-nine, he raised a glass to mark the seventy-fifth anniversary of the shop's tenure in the town, as a special guest of the shop manager at the time. He was always so proud of being M&S's first customer in Dewsbury!

The history of Beaumont and Blackburn goes back almost a hundred years. My father Edward Harper Blackburn, who was known to everyone as Teddy, started the business as a sole trader in 1920. Later in the decade he was joined by Mr Ernest Beaumont, at which point the business became a limited company. Prior to moving to the arcade, the company had a shop on Church Street at the site where the Agricultural Supplies shop would later be opened.

I left school in 1952 at the age of sixteen to work in my father's company as an apprentice electrician and spent ten years 'working on the tools', as undergoing your training was called in those days. The main business of the company was always in electrical contracting work, which at that time mainly involved working in the local mills. It was my father who was particularly keen on the retail side of the business. I think he had always dreamed of owning a shop!

Mr Beaumont was a lot older than my father and died in 1948. It was not long after that my father decided to open a shop in the arcade. Beaumont and Blackburn opened its doors in the arcade in the early 1950s, at around the time that I started my apprenticeship, and occupied the units at the left-hand side of the Market Place entrance, which had previously been used by the Yorkshire Electricity Board.

The southern façade watches over a bustling 1950s town centre. At the left-hand side of the entrance is Beaumont and Blackburn Electricals, established during the post-war period by Teddy Blackburn. On the right-hand side of the entrance is the legendary Ann's Pantry, purveyors of the best Eccles Cakes in Dewsbury.

The shop offered a wide range of products. We did a particularly good line of light fittings but also sold larger white goods such as washing machines, electric cookers and dryers as well as smaller electricals like lamps, irons, kettles and toasters (I remember that the shop was very narrow, which made it really difficult to move and display large items like washing machines and electric cookers etc, but we managed somehow). We sold all the little electrical bits and pieces like torches and fuses too. Electrical items in those days were all sold without a plug, which you had to put on yourself, so we did good business in selling plugs as well. A man called Tom Crowther was the shop manager and chief salesman.

The shop was a thriving concern for a number of years. There were quite a lot of reasonably wealthy people in Dewsbury at that time, and many were on good wages. We did brisk business, especially on a Saturday. If you didn't do much trade on a Saturday, it was a really bad do! However, some people couldn't afford to buy big electrical items like washing machines in a single transaction in those days, so many customers bought on 'hire purchase'. We used a company called Mercantile Credit to offer this service, although it cost the customers a bit extra to buy on credit of course. We didn't do rentals though. You had to go somewhere else for that.

The shop had two sales floors and a third floor which we used to do repairs (the cellar, however, was less useful, as it was often ankle deep in water!). It's a throw-away society nowadays, and it often costs more to have something repaired than to buy a new replacement, but at that time it was always cheaper to have your faulty items repaired. We used to repair heaters, electric fires, TVs and toasters etc. We also did contract work through the shop, going out to customers' homes to fit cookers, washing machines and light fittings etc, mostly in the local area.

I was never particularly interested in the retail side of the business and nearly always worked on the electrical contracting side, working out of the main company office at 21 Wellington Road. In fact, I took over that side of the business from my father in the mid-60s and continued to manage this area until I retired in 2000. After doing lots of contract work in the mills in the early days, we moved on to working in schools and hospitals, often in the Doncaster and South Yorkshire area. Later, we spread our wings wider, working in such places as Torquay and Aberdeen. We even did four or five jobs in Denmark, fitting out a number of small shops with computers etc.

A soot-blackened southern façade watches over Market Place in the 1960s. Beaumont and Blackburn's boasts new signage, though Ann's Pantry is as familiar as ever.

Dewsbury was a lovely, thriving town in the 1950s and 1960s, with lots of lovely shops. It was great for clothes, and you could buy anything you might want to wear, like smart suits and jackets and ties. There were lots of ladies' fashion shops too. Nobody had to go to Leeds, like many do now. The arcade was very smart at that time too. I remember Ballance's flower shop, which was just across the Market Place entrance from B&B. Later, this became Ann's Pantry. I remember Forrest's, Auty's Music Shop, J&B's and Ivor Burns shoe shop. I particularly remember that there was a grocer's shop at the top-left hand side of the arcade. My wife's brother used to work there, and I remember him cutting huge slabs of butter, in the days before everything came pre-packed.

I remember one occasion in 1954, when my father struck lucky for a second time. He was the Chairman of the Chamber of Trade at that time, and President during that particular year. It was in this role that he was chosen to meet The Queen and The Duke of Edinburgh on the occasion of their visit to the town, shaking their hands with pride.

In the late 1960s the shop came under increasing competition and struggled to stay competitive. The growth of the electrical giant Comet and the establishment of out-of-town shopping centres was a double blow. Eventually, we closed the shop. I think it was in 1967! My relationship with the arcade didn't end there, though!

In 1969, with the electrical contracting side of the business still thriving, we bought Shepley's, a plumbing and decorating firm that had been in the town for a long time, but which had recently been in financial trouble. Beaumont and Blackburn at that point became plumbers, decorators, heating engineers and electrical contractors (we soon got rid of the decorators though, as they were a lazy lot!). Shepley's had a shop on Bond Street, but it didn't sell much and shut soon afterwards. The contracting side remained busy, though. Building companies often found it useful to employ just one company to complete lots of finishing off jobs, so we benefitted from that.

It was in this role that the company was contracted to complete some repairs to the roof of the arcade. The arcade was owned by a London company at the time, and they weren't the best in terms of maintenance. We did some repairs to the guttering, which were cast iron. We replaced like for like, installing new cast iron guttering rather than the plastic which had become popular. We also did some repairs to the glass in the roof, installing safety glass to replace damaged sections. It's funny that I've been asked to share my memories of the shop, as it's these repairs to the roof that I remember most clearly.

Eventually, in the year 2000, and having worked at Beaumont and Blackburn for 49 years, I retired. My son-in-law ran the business for a further 6 years, but it was finally wound up in 2006.

There were some good times and some bad times during my working life at Beaumont and Blackburn, but overall, I enjoyed it. Dewsbury was a great place then. I'd love to see the arcade restored to its former glory. It's such a lovely building with lovely frontages. It would be nice to have a good reason to go to Dewsbury. There's not much there for me anymore, as the town has suffered a lot from internet shopping I suspect. I only go there to have my haircut now. They can't do that online!

Memories of Beaumont and Blackburn Electricals
by June Sykes

I worked at Beaumont and Blackburn in the early 1960s. During the week I worked at the company offices on Wellington Street but on Saturdays I worked in the shop, which was on the left-hand side of the southern entrance to the arcade – Number 23 Market Place. I liked working Saturdays in the shop as it gave me a bit of extra money, and I liked meeting and talking to people too – I still do!

The shop sold electricals, mostly white goods like washing machines but also things like toasters, hand-held food mixers and electric carving knives, which were a status symbol at the time. We didn't sell TVs or radios though, as it wasn't that kind of a shop. In fact, the company's main business was as electrical contractors and in electrical installations etc. The shop was a bit of an added extra really.

It wasn't the busiest of shops, as electricals weren't the kind of thing that people bought regularly in those days. It was a lovely, friendly shop, though it was quite formal too, with very high standards. All the shop staff had to be well-dressed and smart, and the girls all had to have nice make up. I remember particularly that the manageress (her name escapes me, unfortunately) was always immaculately dressed and invariably wore impeccable make-up. Unlike me, she worked full-time in the shop. She was a very nice woman!

The customers in the shop were often quite 'well to-do'. Not everyone could afford to buy washing machines and such like in those days. In fact, very few people came in and bought expensive items outright. Most customers bought on hire purchase, which the manageress would process the paperwork for.

One of my favourite memories of working in the arcade is of buying my dinners at Bailey's Café. It was quite a tradition for arcade staff to buy their dinners from Bailey's. You could order your meal and it would be served on a plate with a plate on top and with both plates wrapped in a tea towel. You would collect it from a special window. I would usually take mine back to the shop and eat it upstairs. Then I would wash the plates and take the plates and tea towel back to the café.

On other occasions we would go to sit in the café itself, which was originally located upstairs (later, the business moved downstairs into the former John Colliers shop). I remember Miss Bailey very well. She was always so well-dressed. She would stand behind the counter and barely lifted a finger. She would keep her eye on the money, though! It was such a popular place. Sometimes they were queuing down the steps! The food was lovely! I remember having steak pie, cabbage, peas and mash. Or sometimes it was carrots instead of peas.

The arcade was so lovely in those days. It had a very

Victorian feel about it, as if you were going back in time. I often wondered what it would have looked like 60 odd years earlier, with all the customers in Victorian dress. It looked very atmospheric and authentic. It was quite narrow, though, and it was a tight squeeze if you had to negotiate a pram or two. There were some great shops in the arcade, like Auty's Music Shop, Ivor Burns shoe shop, Walco Leather Goods and John Laing's menswear. For some reason, I always liked to walk up the arcade. I don't think I've ever walked down it!

Dewsbury was always so busy in those days, especially on Wednesdays for the market and on Saturdays. People used to travel from all over to come to the town. There were regular coach trips from across the county, especially on a Saturday. If I had my dinner in Bailey's on a Saturday, I would often get talking to someone from York or Skipton or Scarborough. They had usually come to Dewsbury especially for the shopping!

When I look back on those days, I realise that we didn't fully appreciate what we had. If we could get the arcade back again, it would be absolutely thrilling!

If I had to put my feelings about those days into writing, I would only need one word – fabulous!

6

☙

Ivor Burns Shoes

Memories of Ivor Burns Shoes (and a lot more!)
by Ivor Burns

I've always been an ambitious person, and I've never been afraid of taking a risk. After all, you have to speculate to accumulate! Even at the young age of 16, I had a good business head. I remember my dad, Tommy Burns, having a good friend called Granville Exley who had an ice cream works in Batley Carr. I agreed to help out there, unloading the ice. I must have been a good worker, because he soon offered me a proper job.

Before long, I noticed that there was a spare room in the building. It was then that I had an idea. I would start up my own ice cream business! It was called 'Granny's Ices'. A friend called Jocky Clegg worked there with me. He would boil the mixtures for the cream, and I would often stay up all night on a Friday, making the ice cream. Then on the Saturday I would push my cart along Bradford Road and set up stall in the Market Place in Dewsbury. On a good Saturday, I would take far more money in a day than the average person would earn in a week, which was around £5.00 at that time. So, I didn't do too bad!

The Second World War had recently ended, and rationing was still very much in place, including the rationing of sweets. So, as you can imagine, ice cream was a very popular option. The pitch I had on the Market Place was a real money spinner, although I wasn't legally supposed to be trading from there. Hence, I often had a visit from PC49, who would give me a ticket for illegal trading. I would go to court and would have to pay a fine of £5.00 but within two weeks I was back in the same spot again. Of course, I got another visit from PC49, and I had to pay another £5.00 fine, but the takings on a Saturday were far greater than the £5.00 fine, so it was well worth the visit to court!

Before long I had set on four hawkers, one of whom was an old school friend called Arthur Stringer. Each had their own cart, and each had a set route where they would trade from, be it in Dewsbury Market Place, on Dewsbury Moor or up Thornhill. Even though I was building up a good reputation, I couldn't compete with 'The Cadamarteri Family'. If their cart pitched up, you had no chance!

I did get a job offered by Joey Caddy on one occasion, and also from his brother Johnny on another, which I accepted. Johnny made ice cream out of a little yard at the end of Warwick Road in Batley Carr, and I agreed to take the cart out, but only on a few occasions.

The ice cream trade was a cut-throat business at that time, so it was always nice when you 'got one up' on your competitors. Back then ice cream was mostly sold in paper, as wafers were hard to come by. On one occasion I managed to get my hands on a job lot of Huntley and Palmer's best wafers. I sold the wafers to Caddy's for 25 bob a tin! I also took another 250 tins across the Pennines to sell to 'Granelli's' in Blackpool. It was safe to say that I made a killing!

Caddy's closed their doors in the 1980's, I think. The chap that made the ice cream, John Crossley, obviously knew the recipe for the ice cream, so I asked him if he wanted to go into business with me by opening a little parlour, but he wasn't interested.

My career in the ice cream trade was soon cut short because in 1947, at the age of 18, I began my two and a half years of National Service. I was stationed just outside Hamburg. In the following year, the Berlin Airlift began. This was when the new communist East German Government closed the land route across East Germany to the pro-Western enclave of West Berlin within the old capital. All food and other products had to be flown into West Berlin from West Germany, across East German airspace. It was one of the biggest crises of the Cold War.

Much of this time I was working under the Americans, helping to load the planes. There was lots of food and other products knocking around at that time (chocolate, sweets, cigarettes, etc). The Americans had loads of the stuff!

Whilst in Germany, I have to admit that I did dabble in the black market a bit! All the city's dealers and hawkers would hang around Hamburg's Winklestrasse. I knew them all. Of course, I didn't trade with stolen goods. I just used to barter or sell the stuff from our allowances that we were legally allocated as serving troops. Our allocation was 110 cigarettes. These were given on a regular basis. As well as my own allocation, I would buy cigarettes from any of my mates who didn't smoke. These were easily swapped on the black market. I could swap five cigs for a watch, or three would get you enough beer for a good night out.

The Kiel Canal area was also known for hawkers. I knew that five cigs were the going rate for a watch, but only I wanted to give four! Anyway, on one occasion I went along a line of hawkers to see if anyone would accept my reduced offer. Initially I had no takers, until I eventually came across one who took the bait. The deal was done! Unfortunately for the hawker, I heard a splash while I was walking away. He had been thrown in the water by his disgruntled mates!

The City of Hamburg is a beautiful place and a great city for a night out. I really enjoyed my time there. It wasn't a place that you could go to every day, though. You were supposed to have a pass to travel into the city, but if you know the ropes, you could get away without one.

On one occasion, because we didn't have a pass, myself and a couple of Irish friends decided to thumb a lift into the city. A couple of times we had to dive into a ditch to avoid the Redcaps - The Military Police. Eventually, a long black limousine pulled up in front of us. We clambered in and I immediately noticed that the passenger that was being chauffeured was wearing a dog collar. He asked us lots of questions about our time in Germany (was it hard work? was the food good? etc). When we reached the city, and after saying our goodbyes, my friend asked me if I knew who the mystery passenger was. I said that I didn't, and he told me that it was the Archbishop of Canterbury. 'He's a nosey bugger, isn't he?' I replied.

The German mark was more or less worthless in the years following the Second World War, so the money that I had made on the black market was pretty much worthless too. As I was about to return to the UK, I was facing a major conundrum. I couldn't risk taking the money back myself, as there was no way I could have made all that money just by drawing my regular salary in Germany. I couldn't share it out with my friends either, because one of them could have let it slip as to where it had come from. So... I just burnt it all!

Before I knew it, I was back in Yorkshire looking for a job. I tried my hand at tailoring, but that didn't suit me (excuse the pun!). In the early 1950s, I saw a job working in the shoe repair section within the Batley Co-op. I applied, got the job, and within 18 months I became the foreman. I had found something that suited me.

It was at around this time that I was walking through Birstall town centre one day. I noticed a little shop at the end of the town, opposite St. Patricks Catholic Church. I thought it looked like a good prospect and, as it was for sale, I decided to buy it. It cost me £200. This was to be the first of my many shoe shops.

I had the Birstall shop for about four years. During this period, I first saw the potential in trading on Dewsbury Market. One day I was stood next to a business associate, Margaret Twigg, and was watching as she counted her day's takings from the market. I decided that it must be worth having a go.

At first, I sold carpets, buying job lots and by weight. Two of my sisters made the carpets into rugs, which were our main source of trade. I converted some old K29 sewing machines into electric machines. These were used to cut the carpets and finish the rugs.

It was quite hard to get a market stall at that time. Some potential traders had to wait twelve months before they could get a stall. However, before long I had four stalls together, selling rugs. I sold them for twenty-five bob apiece. It was a roaring trade. My mum looked after the Birstall shop, my wife Margaret helped out in the arcade shop, and I worked on the market. Eventually the Birstall shop got pulled down to make way for the new St Patricks Church.

Our little empire was a real family business. We were three brothers and three sisters, all living on Howard

Street in Batley Carr. We had a warehouse three doors
down from our family home. A friend called Ernest
Tong worked in the warehouse. Another friend that
played an important role was Seth Hoddy. I had a credit
round at that time around Birstall, for which I used my
Morris Minor. Seth bought me a van, which made things
a lot easier.

Around 1960 is when my relationship with the Arcade
began. The D. Douglas Shoe Shop had been in the
arcade from day one. At the time the shop was managed
by Dorothy Douglas, although it was Mr Douglas who
approached me on Dewsbury Market to see if I wanted
to buy the business. Like I said before, I>ve always been
ambitious, so I decided to go for it!

Before long Ivor Burns Shoes had taken up residence
in the arcade. We were based in three units close to the
bottom end of the arcade, on the right-hand side as you
walk down: 5,7, and 11, (unit 9 was a toilet). Dorothy
Douglas stayed for a while, though initially the place was
run by a manageress.

The business that we inherited sold different styles of
shoes and at different prices, including the cheaper
variety. However, we decided to replace the cheaper
ranges in the shop and sell only the better-quality
leather styles.

I still remember the brand names today. We sold
Elmdales, Equity court shoes and Freed's ballet shoes,
with their stiff toe. They were a good quality option. We

also sold shoes for the discerning ballroom dancer. In the men's section we sold varieties like Sargents, Loakes, Padders, Hampton's and Stirling and Hunt, along with Richard Draper sheepskin and lambswool boots and slippers. We had our own brand of shoes, too. I would buy left over lengths of leather from the manufacturers and design the shoes myself. The design would be sent off to our factory to be made up under our own brand name. If you had your own shoes made up, you could sell them at a cheaper price and still make a profit.

The window display at Ivor Burns Shoes. Ivor bought the business from the Douglas family sometime around 1960, though officially he continued to trade as D. Douglas Ltd, a name which would be associated with The Arcade for one hundred and eleven years.

Over the years the family shoe business continued to grow. At one point I had a stall on Dewsbury Market, a shop in the arcade. a shop in Halifax, two units in Kirkgate Market in Leeds and a factory shop in Pudsey.

I remember the 1970s - that decade was a very lucrative time!

Eventually though, Ivor Burns Shoes went the same way as most of the other businesses in the arcade. Lots of people think that when the town lost Marks & Spencer, that was the turning point in the fortune of the town. For me though, it was the pedestrianisation of the Market Place. In the days when the road passed in front of the Market Place entrance, a pedestrian crossing directed you straight into the arcade. As a result, the arcade remained a well trodden route between the bus station and Dewsbury Market. Following pedestrianisation, though, people started to take different routes, and the footfall in the arcade began to decline.

It was at around this time that the arcade was taken over by new owners. The arcade started to suffer from poor maintenance, and in my opinion that's when businesses started to suffer too. There were still some great shops in the arcade, though. Shops like Auty's Music Shop, John Laing's menswear and Candyman. However, businesses slowly started to move out of the arcade and set up shop in places like Ossett, though some are still in Dewsbury to this day.

I finally decided to turn over the closed sign in the arcade, I think it must have been in 2009, or perhaps 2010. At least half of the units were empty when we came out, and the arcade was on a downward spiral. I continued to run the shops in Halifax and Pudsey, and of course we still had the stalls in Dewsbury and Leeds Markets, which

I was helped in running by my son, Richard. Eventually, the Leeds stalls had to be closed down too. Richard took over the running of the Dewsbury Market stall and is still trading there today. It would be a real shame if the market ever went away, as we have been trading there for around 60 years.

About 6 years ago, at the age of 87, I finally decided that after working for 70 years plus, I perhaps ought to retire. I'd probably done enough!

7

🎋

Café Gio / Bennetto's

Memories of Café Gio
by George Alexander

I was the proprietor of Cafe Geo, which was located at the right-hand side of the Corporation Street entrance to The Arcade in Dewsbury. It was a very busy café, so much so that I employed six people at one time. The café was always heaving on market days, which were extremely busy from 8am right through to 4pm. The other days were mainly busy in the morning, mostly with people buying a takeaway coffee before they caught the train.

The cafe was the first of its kind in Dewsbury. It was a very cosmopolitan café, and we had a mix of everyone coming in: Bosnian, Albanian, Italian, Asian, English. You name them and we had them!

Dewsbury was a friendly town in those days and people always looked out for each other. The atmosphere in the arcade was always good, too. I had tables outside the café, which people always liked to sit at. On occasions I would have music nights when we would have singers performing, and these would often draw great crowds. I had an alcohol licence, so it felt like a proper night out for people.

There was a great atmosphere in my café, too. In fact, my business was more like a friendship café. People from all walks of life would come in and make friends with the other customers, and I sometimes felt like a counsellor! Working conditions were mostly okay. The arcade needed lots of work doing to it though, but sadly this never happened.

There were a few memorable events during my time at the arcade. I remember one occasion when Michael Heseltine's wife came in for coffee. The funny thing was the amount of secret service men that were checking the café out beforehand – the place looked like something from a James Bond film! We had Tony Robinson come in for a coffee once too, which was good.

The arcade was a great place at that time. I particularly remember that the Candyman shop was always very busy. I loved my time in the arcade! The town started declining though when Marks & Spencer closed down. That's when my turnover made a big decline, and it was the beginning of the end for my time at the café.

Memories of Bennetto's Café
by Steve Seller

I first started working in Bennetto's towards the end of 2010. The name of the café was an Italianised play on the name of the owner at the time, Dennis Bennett. Dennis was quite a character. The arcade had something of a pigeon problem at the time, and Dennis had his own method of tackling it. He would come down early in the morning with his air rifle and simply shoot them! I remember one occasion when he shot a pigeon and it landed on top of one of the lights and burst into flames!

I had recently been made redundant and was looking for a new challenge. I worked under Dennis for a few months, as I wanted to learn the ropes and familiarise myself with the way the café was run, eventually buying the business in February 2011. I agreed to stick with the name Bennetto's though, at Dennis's request.

The café was a thriving business in the early years. We were a typical café in many ways, selling sandwiches and paninis etc. We had about ten covers downstairs, where we served coffee and cakes, and about twenty covers upstairs, where we served meals out of the kitchen. We certainly got plenty of exercise running up and down those stairs!

When I first started there were three people working in the café and it turned over about £500 a week, but before long we were turning over more than a grand a week and I had to employ another person. The place was always rammed and had a real buzz to it. We had a great crowd of regulars, some of whom are still with me now. Occasionally we would open in the evening to host spiritualist events etc. The café was open from as soon as I got there in the morning (which was always early) until 5pm, Monday to Saturday. They were great days, and I was a lot busier that I am now!

The arcade was a great place at that time too. There were some nice people that worked there and some great little businesses. There was a record shop, a flower shop, a sweet shop, a tobacconist, an arts and crafts shop, a Polish shop and even a solicitor's office. The arcade always looked lovely at Christmas, when we held a festive market, and everyone made a big effort with the decorations. The arcade had a lovely 'oldy-worldly' look about it, though it wasn't very well maintained.

I worked with some great people during my time at the arcade. I remember one particular lad called Paul Wilkinson. He had worked under Dennis, and I inherited him as an employee when I bought the business. He was a bit of a lad about town. On one Sunday morning, when I came in to clean up, I found him fast asleep on the sofa upstairs. He'd had a good night, but I got the shock of my life!

Prior to Dennis owning the business the café was run by George Alexander. Apparently, when George had the café, it was absolutely kicking and regularly hosted musical events etc. I tried to recreate some of that atmosphere by applying for a drinks licence. I just wanted to sell a continental lager and a bit of wine, but there were too many hoops to jump through. I do recall a time though when a group of Albanian builders were working in the town. They used to come into the café before work, bright and early in the morning, and I have to admit that they often had a cheeky shot of ouzo with their espressos.

Eventually, due to the behaviour and attitude of the landlords, all of the tenants left the arcade and the businesses all closed. The landlords were always keen to collect their money, but they weren't so keen on maintenance etc. They didn't even clean the arcade. There was a cleaner at one time, but even though he was only paid £150 per month, they sacked him! At one point I even offered to clean the arcade myself, in exchange for a £150 per month reduction in my rates, but they made it sound like it was me that was asking them for a favour! As a result, the arcade became really dirty, and there were pigeon droppings everywhere. Sometimes the street cleaners would make their way through to give the place a quick once-over, though I'm pretty sure that they weren't supposed to.

Finally, towards the end of 2015, and after over five years of working in the arcade, I threw in the towel, as did everyone else. The rent was approaching £9000 per annum at the time, and it was becoming increasingly difficult to be profitable. The tenants all had to pay a £3000 bond upon taking a lease, but everyone had difficulty getting it back. I left owing six month's rent, so I got mine back that way. In the end, the landlords were responsible for everyone leaving. I was the last man standing, and the café was the last business in the arcade to close its doors.

I moved my business to its current location in Empire House, just opposite the Town Hall. It's quieter now, as some of the offices are still empty after the pandemic. I still have all my regulars though, some of whom have been with the café since George's time. My current place suits them better I suspect, as some of them are knocking on a bit so their glad they don't have to tackle the stairs. It's a shame that the arcade café had to close, though. It was such a wonderful arcade, and in a great location right in the heart of the town centre. There's still a Pizza oven of mine upstairs in the café too. I wouldn't mind it back, actually!

8

✤

Forrest's

Memories of Forrest's Fancy Goods Shop
by Richard Bott

Our family's relationship with Forrest's was formed
between the wars when my dad's sister Rose (born 1889)
married Robert Forrest. My dad Frederick (Fred) Bott
was born in 1903. He married my mum Marjorie (nee
Rigg) before the Second World War and their first
house was just off Bennett Lane in Hanging Heaton. As
a boy my dad had lived on Slaithwaite Road in Thornhill
Lees. He was one of nine children, having seven sisters
and one brother. He must have joined Forrest's before
the war started, but I am not entirely sure when. Prior to
that he had worked in engineering. He occasionally used
to talk about having worked at Armstrong Siddeley, the
luxury car manufacturer and aircraft engine maker.

During the war my mum and dad had to move to
Grantham in Lincolnshire. Because of his engineering
background, my dad was sent to work making guns for

Spitfires! He worked for the British Manufacture and Research Company (BMARC), which specialised in making aircraft cannon and naval anti-aircraft cannon. They were based at a remote location in the Springfield Road area of the town, a similar setting to many other sites around the country. This was part of a planned government strategy to avoid too much concentration of war production in one particular area. The Grantham BMARC plant produced over half of the total number of Spitfire cannons made during the war, a fact of which my dad was very proud. Along with this he also served in the local Home Guard. I am very proud of his contribution to the war effort.

I was born in Grantham in 1941 and my sister Susan was also born there in 1944. After the war the family returned to Dewsbury, moving to a house on Windermere Road in Hanging Heaton, not far from Mum and Dad's pre-war home. Uncle Bob and Auntie Rose lived close by in Bennett Lane. Dad soon returned to Forrest's and, with Uncle Bob and Auntie Rose approaching retirement, gradually took over the management of the shop again. In retirement Uncle Bob and Auntie Rose lived in Scarborough for a number of years before returning to Dewsbury and buying a bungalow on Ullswater Road – in Hanging Heaton!

I believe that Forrest's was one of the original shops in the arcade and had been there from the very beginning. It was based in units 16 to 22, though where it was prior to this I do not know. There must have been a shop somewhere in the town though, as I remember the headed paper that was used in the 1950s which boasted that it had been 'Established Over Ninety Years'. My dad was involved in the business for 40 years or more. My mum worked there too as well as my sister Susan, who joined the perfumery department on leaving school. As I remember there were around four shop assistants, and it was a real family business where everyone helped each other and cared for one another.

Susan Clow (nee Bott) and Marjorie Bott in the very well-stocked perfumery at Forrest's. Marjorie's husband Fred was the store manager during a thirty-year period following the Second World War.

Since before the war, the shop had sold a wide range of quality products. It was often thought of as a 'fancy goods' shop and was the kind of place that people would often go to for birthday and Christmas presents. It sold gloves, handbags, wallets and purses. Parker Pens were a popular line, as everyone seemed to give and receive them for birthdays and Christmases in the 1960s and 1970s. It sold fine ceramics too, including the popular Beswick Horses. It also sold costume jewellery, including pieces designed by the famous Norman Hartnell. It sold pearls as well and offered a pearl restringing service. I remember that it cost extra to have your string knotted between each pearl so that they would remain in place and so that they wouldn't all scatter everywhere if you broke the string.

The best sellers, though, were probably the perfumes. We sold all the top brands such as Lancome, Yardley and Helena Rubenstein. A particular popular line was called 4711. This is a traditional German perfume made by Maurer and Wirtz that has been made in Cologne since at least 1799. Because it is produced in the city, it is one of the few perfumes that can rightly be referred to as Eau de Cologne. My mum always said that Christmas Eve was an incredibly busy day at the perfumery. Most of the menfolk would finish work at lunchtime on Christmas Eve. Naturally, their first port of call was always the pub. It was only after a few pints that they belatedly decided that they might have to buy a Christmas present for the wife! At this point they were easy targets, and my mum said that it was always child's play to shift lots of expensive box sets of perfumes and cosmetics later in the afternoon on Christmas Eve. Served them right!

My dad was the manager of Forrest's in the arcade for

a good thirty years. The arcade was extremely popular for the whole of this period, and it was something of a heyday. J&B's was a very popular department store, and its upstairs toy department rivalled Forrest's for the number of customers at Christmastime. Then there was Auty's Music Shop of course, which was resident in the arcade for the whole of my dad's time there. Not forgetting Ann's Pantry, which was one of many fine bakeries and confectioners in the town. Beech Tree was a popular spot for tabards, pinnies and overalls too.

The arcade was a very friendly place at that time. Everyone knew each other and looked out for each other. There was a great atmosphere, and everyone made an effort to keep things looking nice. My mum had somehow got hold of the Union Jack that had been raised in the Market Place to mark VE Day. She used to put it up in the shop every year to mark the anniversary.

Dewsbury was a thriving little town at that time too. Wednesdays and Saturdays were particularly busy days, when coachloads of shoppers would be dropped off in the town centre for market day. Tuesday was the quietest day due to the half-day closure. After closing early, my dad would often pop into the Scarborough pub in the Market Place on a Tuesday lunchtime for a quick half.

I have very fond memories of Forrest's and thinking about it makes me feel very nostalgic. It was a super shop with a great reputation and was very highly thought of by the townsfolk of Dewsbury. People still remember it fondly, I believe, even though it closed in 1975.

An incident in the late 1980s just about sums it up for me. I had the pleasure of meeting Mr Lyles, the Lord Lieutenant of Yorkshire, who was essentially the Queen's representative in the county. When I introduced myself, he made a comment about my unusual surname. When I confirmed that I was in fact the son of the renowned proprietors of Forrest's, he made a remark I shall always remember.

'To think you are the son of the splendid Mr and Mrs Bott!' he said.

Memories of Forrest's
by Ruth Tolson

I started working at Forrest's in the early 1970s. Fred Bott was in charge of the main shop, which sold leather goods, pottery, glassware and jewellery. I remember Sandra Dawson, who taught me how to dress the large window displays and the display in the little side window by the middle door, which always had purses, wallets and other small items in. I loved doing the window displays with her and we remained friends until her death some years ago. There was a girl called Angela who worked with us too, and at Christmas and other busy times someone called Edwina helped out as well. Marjorie Bott was in charge of the little perfumery and make up department, assisted by her daughter Susan. I can still picture a particular girl who worked there as well as a young lady who left to work abroad, I think. Upstairs was the stock room, which was like a maze until you got your head round it. The staff room was upstairs, too. You had to be fit to run up and down those stairs at breakneck speed, so as not to keep the customer waiting. I recall that all the shops in the arcade shared toilet facilities at the top of some stairs and above one of the shops. At Christmas time all the staff got a free Christmas dinner at Bailey's Café. Sadly though, we had to go individually as the shop was so busy during the week in the run up to Christmas.

The shop sold Beswick animals, which were very popular. If a Beswick horse got damaged Mr Bott would carefully restore it and sell it to me at a discounted price. I bought one at a much-reduced price to give to my sister-in-law, who was horse mad! The shop also sold those little Hummel figures and the very popular Denby pottery. A Denby coffee set was given to me as a wedding gift by the Bott family and all the rest of the staff. We also sold costume jewellery and pearls and a regular customer came and bought her earrings from us. She was a club singer and told us some tales that had us giggling about her escapades. The leather purses and wallets were kept in drawers and the handbags were displayed on shelves. I still have the one handbag that I bought from there. It was very expensive, even with my shop discount! Of course, all of these had to be dusted regularly and the glass cabinets and counters kept spotless as part of our job. I'm not certain, but I think the perfumery department was one of the first places in Dewsbury to sell the popular new aftershave Brut, along with Rubenstein, Estée Lauder and countless others, all in the more luxurious bracket.

The arcade was a lovely place back then, and always so busy and friendly. There were some great shops in the arcade. There was Ann's Pantry at the bottom end, which sold bread and cakes, and across from there was a men›s outfitters. I think John Laing's was in the arcade at that time, too. There was a tobacconist, a sweetie shop, Auty's Music Shop, Beech Tree, which sold pinnies and overalls, and the Scholls sandals shop, which also had a podiatry service. There was Ivor Burns Shoes, a grocery shop and of course J&B's at the top end. No doubt I shall recall some of the others later, after I've done writing this.

Before I worked in this lovely arcade I used to volunteer for Oxfam. When it was Oxfam's turn to have a Saturday collection day, I would stand at the bottom end of the arcade while a friend stood at the top end, by J&B's, and we would 'trap' people in the arcade so they couldn't avoid being asked for a donation. Of course, in those days you could ask for donations, and we always collected so much that we had to go and get new money tins from the organisers.

Sadly, I can't remember all the shops in the arcade, or their names, I can remember the faces of some of people who worked in the arcade shops but sadly cannot recall their names either. I still have lots of special memories, though!

9

℘

Stanley's Fashions

Memories of Stanley's Fashions
by June Carter

I first started working at Stanley's Fashions in the mid-1960s, when I was just 15 years old. I distinctly remember spending my sixteenth birthday working in the shop – that was in 1966! The shop was in the Market Place at that time, and I worked there full-time as a shop assistant. Before long, however, I left to take a job at Freeman, Hardy and Willis, which was one of the town's many reputable shoe shops. Whilst I was at FH&W, the Stanley's Fashions shop moved into the arcade, to a location about halfway up on the left-hand side, opposite Auty's Music Shop. Eventually, I left my job in the footwear trade and ended up going back to Stanley's Fashions, working in the arcade for the first time.

I must have been only 17 when I started working in the arcade shop. I know this because I remember being in the shop when listening to 'Flowers in the Rain' by The

Move, the first song ever to be played on Radio 1 – that was in 1967! My trusty transistor radio was always playing in the shop to provide a bit of background music.

I continued to be employed as a shop assistant, working full-time. The manageress of the arcade shop, however, only worked part-time, and it seemed like I did the lion's share of all the work. Before long, and although I was still very young, I was made manageress of the shop.

The business was owned by two Jewish gentlemen, the Feldman Brothers. One was called Mark and the other Ronnie, but we all referred to them as Mr Mark and Mr Ronnie. They also had a couple of outlets in Leeds, which were their main shops. I clearly remember them driving over from Leeds with a car full of stock. They would park on Corporation Street and struggle down the arcade carrying armfuls of skirts, trousers and tops. They would pick the takings up each time they visited, which had merely been hidden under the counter awaiting their arrival. I had quite a lot of responsibility for a young woman, really. I would ring them to make various arrangements and let them know what had been happening and so on, but otherwise they would just let us get on with it.

I would describe Stanley's Fashions as a general fashion shop, but with quite a modern outlook. The mid to late 60s were the era of the mini skirt, of course, and we sold these in large numbers. We didn't sell dresses, as it wasn't that kind of a shop. Our main lines were 'separates' such as skirts, flared trousers, blouses (at least we called them blouses, though nowadays we would just call them tops), jumpers and cardigans. We were also known for selling lingerie such as corsets, nightwear, nylon stockings and tights. We sold lots of tights, as I remember. Tights only became fashionable at the time of the mini skirt era, when 'clumpy' shoes were also worn. We didn't wear stiletto heels with short skirts in those days. Before that if you wore a dress or a skirt you would be wearing stockings, or 'nylons' as we called them. Women hardly ever went bare legged in those days, unlike today.

We had a lovely glass counter in the shop. It had a number of drawers which were filled with different types of underwear. On the top of the counter sat a mechanical till which rang when you opened it. There were no such things as calculators in those days, so you needed to be able to add up the bill, take the money and give the correct change. Receipts, if asked for, were always hand-written. The shop was open weekdays from 9am to 6pm, though we were closed all day on Tuesdays and obviously Sundays too. Town centre shops were hardly ever open on Sundays at that time.

In the 60s, lots of the young girls in Dewsbury used to work in the mills five day a week. As a result, Friday afternoons and Saturday mornings were invariably busy with mill girls making their weekly purchase. Work was hard in the mills, so the girls had earned their little treat, which probably made their working life a little more bearable. We sold clothes for the older lady, too. They seemed really old fashioned to me at the time, but the ladies who bought them were probably only in their

30s and 40s, which lots of people think of as still being young today.

One thing that fascinates me thinking back is the sizes range that we sold in the shop. The skirts and trousers that we sold only had waist sizes from 22" to 28" and hip sizes from 34" to 40". That is quite small compared to today's sizes. I think the average size for a woman in the 1960s was probably the famous 36, 24, 36. Women and girls were generally smaller in those days.

In the late 60s our bosses the Feldman Brothers opened a wig shop, unimaginatively named 'Stanley's Wig Shop', at the opposite side of the arcade. Wigs had been popular in previous centuries, of course, but had made an unexpected comeback in the swinging sixties. The French designer Givenchy had made wigs popular. He was fed up with the length of time that models had been taking on their hair before strutting their stuff on the catwalk. To save time, he made the models wear wigs, and they took off in the wider fashion world. Also, new synthetic fibres meant that realistic, long-lasting wigs could be mass produced cheaply. Big hair was all the rage in Hollywood, too, and the craze was exported over here for a while too. It didn't last long, though.

The arcade was a lovely place at that time. It was always busy, and I particularly remember it being spotlessly clean. The proprietors would clean the shop fronts and the doorways and there was never any rubbish. There were some great shops in the arcade, too. At the top right-hand side of the arcade was an entrance to J&B's.

This was a great department store. I remember seeing Eartha Kitt in there with her daughter on one occasion. She was no doubt performing at Batley Variety Club. Auty's Music Shop was a great shop too, and always very popular. One of my particular favourites, though, was Ann's Pantry, which sold the best Eccles Cakes in town. The thing I bought most often from Ann's though, believe it or not, was buttered plain teacakes.

One of my good friends, Jenny, used to work nearby at Heughan's Chemist, which was very highly regarded in Dewsbury. Jenny and I went to school together, and we were very close. She would often come round to the shop on a lunchtime and together we would go to the fish shop on Crackenedge Lane. We would buy a bag of chips each and then pop to Ann's to buy a buttered teacake. Then we would go back to the arcade and nip upstairs to our makeshift dining area. At intervals along the arcade there were stairs which led to the first-floor storage area. As our bosses brought all the stock over from their Leeds shop, there was quite a bit of room in our storage area, and we had installed a kettle and created a space to sit and devour our chip butties. It was such a simple lunch, but it's a special memory to me now.

Dewsbury was a thriving town in those days. There were lots of great cafés and shops and, of course, the market. The market was always so busy, with coachloads of shoppers bussed in from out of town on Wednesdays and Saturdays. Jenny and I often frequented Stan's Café on the market. Our favoured option was a Spam sandwich – well done! I even once saw The Searchers having a good nosey around the market, no doubt taking a break from their stint at Batley Variety Club. I'm not sure what they were searching for!

I live in Devon now, but whenever I return to Dewsbury, which is perhaps a couple of times a year, I always take in a visit to the market. I know the market in Dewsbury isn't what it was back then, but in Devon there are very few indoor or outdoor markets, and I very rarely go shopping to a proper market down here. I'd be happy to have something like Dewsbury Market close to me and would definitely be a regular shopper there.

I left Stanley's Fashions in the late 60s. Women married earlier in those days, and many didn't go out to work as most do now. I was one of those women for a while. I enjoyed my time in the arcade though, and those days bring back so many special memories for me.

10

🕭

Johnson & Balmford

A Brief History of Johnson and Balmford (J&B's)

There were many Christmas traditions which were important to the children of post-war Dewsbury, most of which are sadly no longer honoured today. One such tradition was centred on Santa's long-anticipated annual visit to his much-loved grotto in J&B's, the town's famous department store.

Most people of a certain generation will remember J&B's with great joy, recalling how as children, three or four weeks before Christmas Day, they would queue outside the shop in their hundreds to see Santa Claus arriving on his sleigh. Prior to this, many of the same children would have passed their Christmas lists to one of Santa's helpers as the big man passed through the town's suburbs on his 'sleigh', usually a modified flat-bed truck. Upon arriving at J&B's, Santa would climb a ladder to a first-floor window, specially removed for the occasion, and take up residency in his grotto for the festive period. Many recall Santa almost falling off the ladder on a couple of occasions!

The first J&B's store opened in Dewsbury in 1904 and was located on the corner of Market Place and Foundry Street, the first of two locations to be known as 'Busy Corner'. For many subsequent decades the name 'J&B's' was so popular amongst the town's shoppers that no-one would ever have dreamed that such a successful business could ever close down. But, like so many other stores in Dewsbury, including Marks & Spencer, it eventually did!

The firm was founded by a Mr and Mrs James Johnson. The Johnsons brought a partner by the name of Mr N. Balmford into the firm, and so the business became Johnson & Balmford - J&B's.

The first shop was based in the building previously occupied by the C. W. Bunning store. The shop was remodelled in 1908, when most of the walls were removed, a new staircase was added, and new windows were put in. In the mid-1920s, J&B's also took over the shop at the left-hand side of the Market Place entrance to The Arcade, which had previously been Jubb's Tailors. This became J&B's 'Fancy Department', selling robes, blouses, furs, umbrellas and ladies' underwear.

Although the business had expanded to various locations across the town over the years, in 1926 it finally found a permanent home in the four-storey building on the corner of Foundry Street and Corporation Street, at what also became known as 'Busy Corner', as shown in the accompanying photo. The J&B's store on this Busy Corner was much bigger than the town's Marks and Spencer store. Moreover, the business also had a number of other shops across the town at various times as the company gradually expanded and diversified throughout its long history.

J&B's took over Jubb's 'bottom end' store in 1925, the shop becoming the renowned retailer's 'Fancy Department'.

The owners had spent a fortune on the new J&B's, which they equipped with every available modern feature, including an electric lift to all floors. The move to the new location provided an opportunity to expand and extend the shop, which the owners gladly took, despite the high costs.

Announcing the opening in a full-page advertisement in the Dewsbury Reporter, the owners boasted to customers: "We are putting our last penny on you!" To mark the opening, they held a series of mannequin parades, morning, afternoon and evening, at which tea and biscuits were served free of charge. The following were some of the items that were on sale on opening day: coats, costumes, drapery, dresses, silks, men's wear, millinery, neckwear, hosiery, gloves, corsets, blouses, robes, underwear, furs, umbrellas and toys. Customers could also enjoy the delights of the new café. Conveniently, the store could be accessed through a doorway at the top right-hand side of the arcade, though its departments were much bigger than those of the typical arcade shop, of course.

J&B's was a store which believed in advertising and always had the biggest and most prominent adverts in the Dewsbury Reporter, sometimes covering whole pages, and it was also widely advertised on many of the town's trams in the early days.

Its slogan was, 'If you need it, J&B's can supply it', and it certainly lived up to this. Another much-used motto was 'Value for money with the utmost of courtesy'.

Another motto was, 'Bargains for the Multitude!' although J&B's was one store which didn't offer credit. In one advertisement it asked potential customers, 'If you have only so much to spend, make sure you are careful that you spend it to the best advantage'. The advert went on: 'We undertake to save you many a penny in rigging out yourself and your little folks if you rig them out at our stores and be honestly dealt with in every way. Cash mind, no credit whatever, but if you haven't the money at the time, and you see something you like, J&B's will put it aside for you if you – fasten it.'

It sold all the latest fashions, even in smaller items like gloves, and it was proud to declare that its kid gloves were made to 'fit not split', and if they did split, customers were asked to take them back so that the manager could 'see what he could do'. Its kid gloves were lined in silk and sold for 2/6d a pair. It also sold much less expensive gloves 'for shopping in', priced 2d. But its most famous gloves were called Edna and Alarm gloves, which were made of beautiful suede fabrics with gold and silver dome fasteners.

Dewsbury's famous 'department' store really did sell almost everything, and being true to the name, had lots of separate departments selling different kinds of products. Here is a list of its 12 departments – jackets, hats, hosiery, gloves, corsets and underclothing, silks, drapery, household goods, haberdashery, dress goods and blouse materials, lace and children's wear.

J&B's was at the height of its powers before the Second World War, although the fondest living memories of the shop are of the 1950s, a period of economic expansion in the town and across the nation. Eventually, though, and much like Marks and Spencer many years later, the shop succumbed to the pressures from local competitors, the ever-growing trend towards catalogue shopping and, most importantly, the mass overseas production of cheaper alternatives to their products, eventually closing their doors after generations of service to the town.

A somewhat grainy image of the famous J&Bs. Photos of the much-loved department store are very few and far between.

What they said about J&B's

I remember J&B's and the shops downstairs with the seats for the customers. Each shop sold different goods and when you paid the cash went up in a chute to the office upstairs. Then the chute would come back down with your change and receipt.

At Christmas Father Christmas toured all around Mirfield on the back of a wagon collecting Christmas lists in a net from excited children, who were all waiting patiently for him to pass. Then he arrived at J&B's,

where the top floor window had been specially removed, and he would climb up the ladder to the upstairs room where the magical grotto was. The arcade would be all strung with fairy lights. Such magical times for us kids in the 50s. – Jojo Takvam

In the 70s it was at the top of the arcade on the right-hand side as you are walking up. I remember it well, with the Britains toys in the revolving glass case. – Joe Walker

I can remember getting my Subbuteo teams there. – Michael Madden

An early C20th tram, bound for Dewsbury and decorated with several J&Bs advertisements.

I stood next to Eartha Kitt in J&B's once. She was buying her young daughter a wooly hat and scarf set, as it was freezing in Dewsbury at the time. She was appearing at Batley Variety Club at the time. – John Woodhead

J&B's was a wonderland when we were young. It sold everything! – Mark Hunter

I remember J&B's. I worked in the cash office in 1965/66, sending change back down to the counters. Happy days! – Margaret Haigh

I remember walking down a very bustling arcade one Christmas with my husband. We were both singers. It would have been about 1990, although we had both known the arcade from when Santa actually went up the ladder into J&B's and almost fell into the sash window! That would have been about 1958! But anyway, back to wandering up the arcade. Dempster and Lister used to make a loaf called the Speckler Crown. We were on our way to buy one and as it was near Christmas we were singing 'Oh the weather outside is frightful and...let it snow, let it snow, let it snow'. What a lovely place to sing! Don't let the arcade go! – Jan Thurlow

11

⁊ᴆ

Arcade Shorts

A Brief History of Walco Leather Goods

Once a familiar sight in many towns and cities across the North of England, Walco Leather Goods shops and market stalls have now disappeared without a trace. As well as selling a range of other quality products, Walco Leather Stores Ltd was the biggest independent retail supplier of traditional clogs in England.

Born in Halifax in 1888, Willie Walton was initially employed as a bootmaker and repairer. However, after having both served in the First World War, on return to civilian life Willie and brother Charles together with sister Annie formed Walton Bros. and Co. Unfortunately, Charles died in 1923, but Willie and Annie continued to run the growing business.

From their hometown of Halifax, they opened shops across Yorkshire, Lancashire and Cheshire, including the shop in The Arcade in Dewsbury, which opened in 1937. Walco outlets were based in a number of settings, from covered markets and shopping centres to several upmarket arcades.

The business became a limited company in the 1950s, with Willie and sons Charles and Fred acting as directors. The trio were also directors of the manufacturing arm of the business, which made boots, shoes, suitcases, trunks and even footballs, although they continued to produce traditional clogs, though admittedly to a slightly lower standard.

Succumbing to both the more widespread use of synthetic materials as well as the mass production of leather products overseas, the company hit trouble in the early 1990s and was finally dissolved in 1995. The shops are all gone, but people still remember them fondly.

Memories of The Scholl Shop and the Walco Leather Goods shop
by Val Sheard

My earliest memories of the arcade are of my mum, Irene, working at the Scholl Shop, or Dr Scholl's Foot Comfort Service, to give it its full name. This was in the early-70s, when I was in my teens, and when Scholl sandals were all the rage. I later discovered that Scholl footwear is scientifically designed to exercise the muscles in your legs as you walk, improve the circulation and allow your toes to flex between steps - apparently!

The manageress, Maureen Lyons, was a qualified chiropodist - and a fantastic woman! I remember my mum and her visiting the local Women's Institutes to give talks on footcare. My mum loved working there. It was a happy place and there was always a friendly atmosphere amongst the staff and their families. I particularly remember that, on occasional Saturday evenings, straight after work, Maureen and I would head over to watch the Halifax Dukes Speedway Team. Maureen was a big fan! We went to Wembley once or twice too, to watch the speedway finals. It was a tiny shop, and it was a tight knit staff. I recall one time when my mum decided to have a quiet word with one of the shop girls, Karen, whom I knew, to ask her if I smoked. I can honestly say that I didn't!

Scholl had a chain of shops across the country. At some time in the mid-70s they asked my mum to transfer to the Huddersfield branch, but she didn't want to move. Luckily, the manageress at a neighbouring shop, Jean Moseley, whom my mum was friends with, offered her a job a lot closer to home. And so, my mum moved to the Walco Leather Goods shop instead.

Some people remember Walco as being a shoe shop, but it also specialised in wallets, purses, leather satchels, school pumps, leather clogs, shoe segs, etc. I remember local school kids buying their satchels and tennis shoes at the shop before the start of the new school year.

Strange as it sounds, one of my favourite memories of the shop relates to Ben, our much-loved family dog at the time. Ben was a character, so much so that he used to travel around unaccompanied on the buses. The drivers would simply let him on at the bus stop and let him off again in town! He was notorious for running away too. During one escape he turned up at Walco and my mum had to look after him for the rest of the day. In fact, he escaped so often that some of the local kids wised up to it. If they saw him wandering the streets, they would return him straight to Walco, as they knew my mum would give them a little reward - like 5p. It was a nice little earner for them! (My son reminded me recently of how Ben used to meet him from school. Once there was some type of protest at the school and a presenter from the television programme Calendar was interviewing parents at the school gates. I watched Calendar that evening, and our Ben appeared on screen, walking into the school grounds to meet my son).

At the end of the seventies my mum managed to get me a Saturday job in the shop, and I worked there for two or three years. I really liked it! There were always a few social events, and even a staff holiday to Malta. I felt valued and trusted and had a few responsibilities. I remember bagging up the cash at the end of the day and depositing it in the Night Safe at NatWest. They looked after me and they looked after my mum too. She had a company pension, which not everybody had in those days.

There was such a good community in the arcade at the time. Everybody knew everybody else, and we all looked out for and helped each other, like asking each other for change and watching over each other's shops when someone went to the loo. The arcade was always busy at that time, especially on Wednesdays and Saturdays. It was nice and clean, and every shop was smart and well kept. There were some great shops in the arcade, like John Laing, Beech Tree and Candyman. Walco was the biggest though!

An atmospheric image of The Arcade in the 1970s. On the right-hand side is the Scholl Shop, or 'Dr Scholl's Foot Comfort Service', to give its full name.

I loved my time at Walco. It was just like a family. I remember going into the shop to tell my mum I was pregnant. Special times!

Here's an interesting post-script! My mum was called Irene Sheard (nee Irene Hemingway). One of her ancestors, John Hemingway, was at one time the owner of the famed Shibden Hall in Halifax. John bought the property in 1614, his father Robert and his aunt Mrs Crowther (nee Lister) acting as guarantors due to John being legally underage. Unfortunately, all three died shortly after, upon which the property passed to John's sisters, Sibel (born 1605) and Phoebe (born 1608). Both sisters married their cousins, who were in fact both Listers! Sibel married Thomas Lister in 1619 and Phoebe married John Lister in 1625. And the rest, as they say, is history! Phoebe Lister (nee Hemingway) was a direct ancestor of the much-celebrated Anne Lister, of 'Gentleman Jack' fame. To be specific, Anne Lister is my sixth cousin 8 times removed and John Hemingway is my first cousin 13 times removed. Piece Hall in Halifax is therefore not the only historical shopping establishment in Yorkshire with links to the county's most famous gay icon!

Memories of Samaflora
by Sam Hirst

I ran a shop called Samaflora. As it turned out, the shop was one of the last businesses to occupy a unit in The Arcade in Dewsbury. It was a very creative and artistic venture, as everything I sold was handcrafted by myself. The products I sold included a range of paper crafted goods, handcrafted flowers and papercut pictures and artwork. As a small business I only employed myself, but I did have the support of close friends and family.

Sadly, Dewsbury was in decline at the time I was resident in the arcade, with more and more phone shops, vape shops and mini markets opening up. I moved into the arcade as the first tenant under the Dewsbury Pioneers social enterprise. They had a vision to redevelop the arcade but unfortunately the arcade owner at the time put up many roadblocks to stop this happening.

At the time I was a tenant in the arcade we had a cafe and a handknitted baby clothes shop then there was myself. We were the start of a vision for a rejuvenated arcade. A lot of local people were behind us and supported us in the hope that we would once again bring back the arcade to what it had been in past years when it was at the heart of Dewsbury.

As everything in the shop was handcrafted by myself, people could and did come to me wanting personalised gifts and I would happily create something special for them. Also, as a lot of my work was actually created in the unit itself, people could come to sit and watch me work on what they had asked me to make. I had quite a following for that! People liked that they could come and sit and have a cuppa whilst they watched me work. The fact that I also ran Saturday workshops and a kids club where kids could come and enjoy crafts made me quite unique!

Market days were the busiest days for me as people would come out for the market and often pop into the shop as they wandered around town. Saturday was definitely the busiest market day as I also ran taster sessions and workshops on a Saturday, giving people the chance to come along and have a go at various crafts.

The funniest story I can tell you about my time in the arcade is about a very early Christmas. You have to understand that I sell to crafters, with my bespoke ranges of handcrafted flowers being a best seller, so getting ready for Christmas to me always started in June. So, one year I decided that the first week in June would be Christmas in the shop! So out came all the decorations and trees and up they went! This was all done after closing one evening when the arcade was locked up for the night. So, imagine the next morning when you walk past in shorts and tees because it's roasting only to find Christmas trees, fairy lights, carols and mince pies for everyone. It was certainly an entertaining week watching people's reactions!

Unfortunately, when I moved in the arcade had been left empty for quite some time and had been badly neglected by the previous owner. It was in quite a bad state of repair, but the shop owners kept morale high and we worked through it, even when heavy rain caused a burst pipe in my shop and I arrived one morning to over an inch of water in the shop and a lot of damaged stock!

My time at the arcade was towards the end of the last time that it was open to the public. As stated previously, the only other businesses in the arcade at the time were Bennetto's Café and Little Bumps, and we were all successful in our own ways. I loved my time working in the arcade and it was a shame it had to come to an end. It really could be such a beautiful place! It was a shame the previous owner didn't see what it could have been. I remember how nice it was when I was a child and I used to love visiting it with its quirky shops and of course Auty's Music Shop.

From the bottom of my heart, I hope you can breathe new life into the Arcade and make it special again by filling it with independent shops and maybe even create a space to have a pop-up shop. It deserves to be seen and used.

The Great Arcade Tree Robbery
by Malcolm Hirst

In 1965, Dewsbury was hugely different from the town it is now. It was a thriving market town with a diverse and busy town centre. There were five cinemas, a variety of department stores (including Bickers, J&B's, Hodgson's and the Co-op), several well-known shoppers' favourites such as M&S and Woolworths, all the major tailors and every high street bank. The market was known throughout the country, with coach trips visiting the town every Wednesday and Saturday. There was also the renowned ice cream parlour, Caddy's, and numerous restaurants, ranging from good cheap eats to expensive special occasion venues.

There were three covered shopping arcades in the town. There were two named Kingsway and Queensway joining Northgate and Foundry Street and one, much older, linking Market Place and Corporation Street and simply known as The Arcade.

The Arcade was splendidly built and maintained and contained a wide variety of individual shops, with a balcony above also containing business premises. The shops were as diverse as a shop selling knitting wool and kindred items (including patterns and needles), a music shop which sold musical instruments, sheet music and a limited range of records (which was extremely popular) and a flower and garden shop – which is the subject of this story.

Dewsbury at this time had its own police force, its own fire service and its own ambulance service. The County Borough of Dewsbury Police Force was the smallest such force in the country, but it had a fierce pride and served the community with great distinction.

It was into that force in 1963 that a new constable was sworn in. The young man became Police Constable 84, Malcolm Hirst. In 1964 he married Kathleen, the marriage ceremony being the last ever to be conducted at the Salvation Army building, which was in Battye Street, Dewsbury. The happy couple held their reception at the Pioneer Restaurant in Pioneer House, Dewsbury.

In 1965 his beat was in the town centre of Dewsbury. At the time there were three beats covering the town, two covered for 24 hours each day and one for 16 hours each day. In addition, on market days there would be an increased level of cover, including an officer designated to the market, one to enforcing safe parking plus, on pay days, a bank patrol. In the evening of the weekends there would be up to eight or ten officers in town to keep the peace and they were supervised by two uniformed sergeants and a uniformed inspector.

That is the background to this little tale involving P.C. Hirst, a tree, The Arcade and a thief.

One summer's day, the officer in question was on patrol in the town centre (on number eight beat, which covered the end of the town including the Co-op, Northgate and the Market Place). He was in the Market Place, outside what was then the Essoldo Cinema, when he saw a commotion at the entrance to The Arcade. A man ran out of the Arcade carrying a tree, followed by a lady shouting at him to stop. The officer quickly made his way to the scene. The shouting lady said that the man had stolen a tree from the garden shop.

By this time, the man was turning the corner from Market Place into Foundry Street, and the officer quickly set off in pursuit. The chase continued up Foundry Street, with the officer gradually catching up with the man with the tree. As they ran across Corporation Street and continued the chase further along Foundry Street, they reached an area where there were a number of yards at the rear of the shops along Northgate. Suddenly, the man turned into one of those yards. As the yards were all dead ends, the officer knew that he had him. As he followed the thief into the yard, the officer was immediately confronted by a strange sight. Bizarrely, the thief was trying to hide the evidence in a dustbin, which is not an easy thing to do with a twelve-foot tree.

The officer arrested the thief. Because in those days there were no personal radios that constables could use to summon police transport, the officer promptly marched the man and the tree back through the town centre and straight to the Police Station, which was at that time in the Town Hall.

It was there that the story behind the theft was revealed. As it turned out, the thief was a local man of very good standing who had gone to the garden shop to complain about a tree that he had previously purchased that had died. There was a dispute between the man and the shop staff regarding his demand for a new tree and he had decided to help himself, steal a tree, and make off.

He was processed through the system, charged with theft, and released on bail. It was accepted that he should not be put before the Court, and he was issued with a caution for his wrongdoing. Luckily, the whole episode was brought to a satisfactory conclusion without the help of Special 'Branch'.

As the now retired officer is 80 years of age, he looks back with nostalgia to his time on the beat in the centre of Dewsbury and the loss of such icons as The Arcade. It is hard to imagine The Arcade and all the other aspects of Dewsbury ever being recovered, but good luck to those who try!

Memories of Bijoux
by Ann Marie Firth

I got my first job at the age of 16, working on a jewellery stall on Dewsbury Market. After I'd been working there for a while my boss decided to take a unit in The Arcade and asked me if I would go to work in there. This was around 1987-88. The shop was called Bijoux and sold designer and costume jewellery. I worked there with another girl. We had to wear a uniform, which basically consisted of a branded track suit which sported the shop name down each leg and also around the back. We had it in three different colours if I remember rightly.

It was great working in the arcade at that time! All the shopkeepers and staff used to stand in the shop doorways - chatting. There was a great community spirit amongst everyone who worked there. We used to keep an eye on each other's shops, (if someone needed to pop upstairs to use the toilet, for instance, as the individual shops didn't have their own loos!). We used to get each other's dinners from the bakery too so that none of the shops were left unsupervised at lunchtimes. It was usually nice and cool in the arcade too, so it was a good place to shelter from the hot summer sun.

It was always so busy in those days. The market used to attract coachloads of visitors most days each week. These day-trippers would normally have a walk around town before getting back on the coach, so we would be busy in the arcade too. We used to close on Tuesdays though, as this was the 'half-day closing'. Every town had a day in the week when they had to close for half a day. This was because of an old law which said that shop workers were allowed a half day holiday in the week to compensate for the fact that they had to work all day on Saturdays. Some shops in Dewsbury didn't bother opening at all, though, as people often used the Dewsbury half-day closure as a good excuse to have a day trip to a neighbouring town, like Batley or Mirfield. The half-day law stopped soon after anyway.

One regular customer at Bijoux was Alan Barton, of Black Lace and Smokie fame. He used to come in the shop most weeks and he sometimes spent a fair bit of money, or it was a lot of money in those days anyway! He was a very friendly fella!

There were some very memorable events in the arcade in those days. I remember when the arcade was renovated. A man everyone knew as Zen was in charge. All the arcade staff had great banter with Zen and the other workers. They re-laid the flagstones and put on the new glass roof. Zen was really nice, and he came round all the shops asking us for our input into the work. He made sure we all got the signs we wanted for outside the shops, for example. Another memorable occasion was the flood. This happened on a Saturday night, so lots of the arcade staff received a phone call the following day to ask them to go in to work to help with the clear up. We were there for most of it, and we were black bright by the end of the day – on a Sunday!!

Coincidentally, my dad, Max Scargill, was hired to

clear the arcade shortly after it closed for the last time in 2016. It was a couple of years later I think, in 2018. My dad was well known locally as the person to turn to if somewhere needed clearing. Most of the stuff was just rubbish for the tip, though he did find some old furniture, a commemorative military medals case and an antique spoon!

The Last 'Reopening'

The last time The Arcade benefitted from a major refurbishment was back in 1987. Much needed at the time, and at a cost of £150,000, the popular thoroughfare underwent a series of significant improvements.

Unsightly modern signs and plastic fascias were removed and replaced with traditional, hand-painted alternatives, complemented by oval, hanging nameboards outside each shop. Decorative window boxes were added to the first-floor windows and ill-fitting fluorescent tube lighting was replaced by more appropriate Victorian lanterns. Electric and telephone cables were hidden from public view and a special gel was applied around the roof areas to prevent pigeons from roosting. The roof itself was completely re-glazed using the original tiles, which had to be numbered to make sure they were put back in the right place. The overall effect was impressive, and the proprietors were pleased with the enhanced look.

The principal contractors were Building and Maintenance Services of Heckmondwike and the main developers were The London Shop Property Group, who boasted that the scheme had 'greatly improved' the arcade's environment.

Mr Clive Coward, a director of The London Shop Property Group at the time, said: 'We have taken great care to restore the original detail of The Arcade, and I believe that the finished result is a credit to everyone involved in the project.'

'We hope that shoppers will enjoy the feeling of days gone by when they visit The Arcade and that the new feel to the development will help them make the most of their shopping.'

The Arcade reopened at 2.00pm on Saturday 28th November 1987, with Mayor of Kirklees Councillor George Speight performing the reopening ceremonies. Arcade traders wore Victorian costume for the day and free hot chestnuts were available for all shoppers. As it was approaching December, many arcade shops adopted a Victorian Christmas theme, encouraging shoppers to join in the fun of Christmases past whilst shopping for Christmas presents.

The full list of shops 'reopening' on the day was as follows (I use inverted commas as The Arcade had actually remained fully operational over the five month restoration period): Just In (fashions), Ann's Pantry, Christine's Florist, Bijoux (fashion jewellery), Healthwise (health food), Beech Tree (overall, pinnies, etc), The Final Touch (perfumes and cosmetics), Walco Leather Stores, Candyman (sweets and tobacco), The Home Video Centre, John Laing (outfitters) and Silks (lingerie). Two other shops welcomed customers on the day too, both of which had stood the test of time and had remained open throughout the entire eighty-eight-year history of The Arcade. They were The Music Shop, trading at that time as C.T. Auty's of course, and D. Douglas Shoe Shop, trading at that time as Ivor Burns Shoes. Both shops continued to open their doors to arcade customers over the subsequent decade and beyond, and both reached the century milestone in The Arcade before turning over the closed signs for the last time in the first decade of this century.

A Proud Musical Tradition

C.T. Auty 'The Music Shop' is quite rightly held in high regard within the town's 'more mature' musical community. Of all the much-loved shops that have graced The Arcade over the years, Auty's very possibly takes pride of place, especially amongst the town's numerous record collectors, many of whom bought their first single or album in the shop.

However, perhaps unknown to many of these former customers, 'The Music Shop' had traded in The Arcade under a different guise for almost as long as it had traded under the Auty's banner and was in fact resident in another location in the town centre prior to The

Arcade opening its doors in 1899.

Auty's was established by Charles and Mary Auty in 1949. Prior to this the store had been owned by Fred Normington and had traded under the name F. Normington 'The Music Shop'. Familiar to the many thousands of the town's residents who bought and owned vinyl records from Auty's, and emblazoned on the shop's instantly recognisable branded sleeves, the suffix 'The Music Shop' had in fact been borrowed by the Auty family from their musical predecessors, (the early Auty's record sleeves identify the shop as 'Late Fred Normington').

Normington's were one of the town's main suppliers of radios and radiograms. They were an authorised dealer for His Masters Voice, providing demonstrations for those who were less familiar with the still relatively new technology.

The early twentieth century was the golden age of radio, with sixty percent of households owing a radio by the 1930s. Radiograms (combined radio and record players built into a cabinet and with a single speaker) were a much newer technology in the pre-war years but became very popular in the late 1940s and 1950s.

Normington's sold a wide range of receivers (radios to you and me), including those produced by Ecko, Ultra, Philips and Marconi. They also sold Hohner, Frontalini, Soprani and Pietro piano accordions. Other popular lines included Trivoice and Ridgmount dance band amplifying equipment, Premier drums and the increasingly popular record tokens, a common birthday gift in the pre-war years.

The recognisable image of The Arcade decorated with bunting for the Coronation of King George V in 1911 clearly shows Numbers 12-14 sporting a familiar His Master Voice dog and horn sign, dating the shop's presence in The Arcade to at least thirty-eight years prior to the establishment of Auty's. Indeed, later Auty's record sleeves and newspaper adverts boasted that the business was 'Established in 1891', confirming the founding of the shop in the pre-Arcade era, and suggesting perhaps that 'The Music Shop' was indeed amongst those shops that had graced The Arcade from the outset.

In the second half of the twentieth century, Auty's was proud to continue to follow this fine musical tradition. The newly named shop was also an authorised agent for His Masters Voice and Columbia radios and radiograms as well as for Decca and HMV Records (the acronym HMV was used to distinguish the recording side of the business from the radio and wider musical equipment side). The same ranges of piano accordions and drums were stocked as under the previous owners, though Challen, Chappel and Eavestaff pianos were also available. Curiously, the shop also sold Rudge and Raleigh Tricycles, some of which were found abandoned in an upstairs room in the 1970s. More appropriately, a piano tuning, reconditioning and instrument repair service was also provided. Later, guitar lessons were also offered. The shop went on to sell a wide range of musical instruments, sheet music and musical related toys.

In the twilight of its years the shop would go on to sell CDs, guitar effects pedals and electronic tuners. Despite the ever-changing technology that informed the range of products that were sold, quality, reliability and value for money were a constant throughout almost 120 years of service to the town, over a century of which was provided from the shop in The Arcade.

12

🙠

The Best of the Rest

Memories of Ann's Pantry
by Deborah Wood

I started working with the company in 1978 and finished working there in 1982. Ann's Pantry was the best place to work! They sold the best confectionery and bread in Dewsbury. Their celebration cakes were amazing and made with the finest ingredients. Their wedding cakes were made to perfection too, and with great attention to detail. All the products in the shop were made in Heckmondwike in their own bakery. The company were famous for their Yorkshire Tea Cakes, which were full of mixed fruit and of a very generous size. I also remember the little Turog loaves which became popular and were ordered in large numbers daily. The window was always decorated so beautifully with them. Not forgetting the Eccles Cakes, of course, which were widely agreed to be the best in town.

A nostalgic image of Ann's Pantry. Barriers protect
any clumsy arcade shoppers from stumbling out into
oncoming traffic.

Ann's Pantry was a Victorian shop with glass shelves
in the windows and old sliding doors to access the
confectionery etc and with an old wardrobe type
cupboard for storage space. The cash register was from
the 1950s, with big white keys, but it was great to have
in the shop. We also made the best sandwiches, with cut
meats from their shop in Corporation Street, which was
also an old Victorian shop until they redesigned it, in
the 1980s I believe. It's a great shame that the business
has ceased trading. I'm sure Dewsbury would be a better
place if it had these types of shops back in the town.

Memories of The Arcade
by Susan Broadbent/Woodcock

I remember going to The Arcade as a young child and picking out my first recorder as a Christmas box gift from Auty's Music Shop. I subsequently visited the shop for many years, buying sheet music for different ability levels whilst learning to play the piano. They would 'order in' whatever sheet music they didn't have in stock, and I couldn't wait for my next piece to arrive. I travelled down from Shaw Cross on the bus with my mum, a shilling in my glove, eager to hand it over, and being careful to not crease the manuscript on the way home!

Ivor Burns was in the arcade for years, selling very good quality (but a tad old-fashioned) shoes. Those were the days when half sizes, width, and even depth of shoe were considered. I especially liked to go at Christmas, when I chose some new slippers with my grandma from the well-stocked window display, which was always decorated with tinsel, baubles and fir cones that were probably kept stored in a box somewhere from year to year.

Ann's Pantry was a very small bakery shop with a very big following. The entrance was at the front of the arcade, but the queue often went half the way up it, and as you got to the inside of the shop, it smelled more and more tempting! It was always our first stop (to beat the queues) and careful stacking of our purchases in the shopping bag was often required in order to eliminate the chance of any unwanted squashing of the buns! My favourite cake was an 'elephant's foot' (a large choux bun filled with cream and laced with chocolate).

The Arcade was my favourite place in town – cool and shaded in summer and a respite from the snow and rain in winter. My special time of year was always the period before Christmas, when the arcade was at its most festive and cheerful, its gleaming well-lit windows shining bright against a dark, cold December day, and the promise of delightful gifts to come...

Memories of The Arcade
By Kath Savage

The cosmetics and handbag shop, Forrest's, was just fabulous! When you went in the smell was intoxicating and the girls working there were lovely and were always happy to help and advise on cosmetics and fragrance. I spent far too much money in there! My boyfriend bought me my first expensive bottle of perfume from there for our first Christmas together – Lancome Envol. My mum loved it too and worked there in the cosmetic department before being called up to do war work. She said Mr Forrest was a lovely man and turned a blind eye to the staff spraying themselves regularly with testers! Her friend worked in the handbag department which sold the brand name of the moment – Waldi. Mum saved up after the war and bought herself a Waldi and had it for years. Mum said that the popular perfumes of the day during the war years were California Poppy, which came in a red bottle, and Evening in Paris, that came in a blue bottle. She also remembers that, during the war, desperate ladies would call in regularly to see if they had received a delivery of Henna, as supplies were becoming very difficult to get. Mum watched as over the weeks the very distressed ladies' hair was showing more and more grey, but there were no supplies to sell!

I remember getting my tap and ballet shoes from Ivor Burns shoe shop – he was the only stockist in town. Then of course there was Auty's Music Shop with their display of musical instruments in one side of the shop and records for sale in the other. Ann's Pantry was at the bottom where Mum always bought us an iced long bun as a treat. I think J&B's had a side entrance at the top the arcade, and that was a great shop, more of a department store really. What a fantastic arcade!

Memories of Auty's Music Shop – 1972
by Jan Thwaites

I worked at Auty's in 1972. I have to admit that I took the job because I really wanted to earn a wage. It was a very enjoyable job because I was into music and got to listen to all the latest chart toppers. I collected all the Motown volumes, which were a particular favourite. I used to love cleaning the instruments in the window and tried them all out. The bagpipes were the hardest to master!

I don't remember too much about the Auty family. Josephine was OK as a boss. I remember her boyfriend coming into the shop to play us a few tunes on his guitar. She liked salt in her coffee, I remember that much! I sold lots of sheet music but can't remember much about the customers who bought it. I sold a few jaw harps, plectrums and recorders too. I remember that Tuesday was half-day and Wednesdays and Saturdays were always busy. The market was thriving at that time and was always bustling with people who came from all over just to spend the day In Dewsbury. My wage was £7.50 per week, but I moved on to a new job for double the wage.

The arcade was always busy in those days. I remember an overall shop opposite, a jewellers at the bottom, Walco shoe shop, a menswear shop at the top and a florist.

Memories of The Arcade
by Judith Wood MBE

My late husband David and I lived in Dewsbury from 1965 to 2017. My earliest memories of The Arcade are from the late 1960s, when we use to go into J&B's department store to visit the toy department on the first floor with our two young sons. I also used to buy shoes from Ivor Burns, where I seem to remember you could buy specialist dance shoes. Other shops I remember were a leather shop selling handbags, purses and wallets etc, a tobacconist, a chemist and a sweet shop, the names of which I cannot recall. But I do recall Christine's Florist and most important of all Auty's Music Shop! I used to go into Auty's regularly, looking through sheet music for old songs to perform in Dewsbury Arts Group's Music Hall Shows. Also, our sons, when in their teens, used to regularly shop for records in Auty's.

The Arcade at some time around the turn of the C21st. The range of shops has changed, though this era is also fondly remembered by many.

The Teddy Boy Era
By Maggie Green

I have some special memories of The Arcade. I was a teenager in the fifties, although teenager wasn't really a word that was used much then. I worked at the co-op at the time, in the office. I have happy memories of Auty's Music Shop.

I think it was probably on Fridays that I used to visit Auty's. Outside the shop they had a glass fronted box which contained all the singles in The Hit Parade. I'd been following The Hit Parade closely for months (The

Hit Parade was the name for the top ten single records, or the 'Charts' as we'd call it today). I'm sad to say that Davy Crockett by Bill Hayes had been in and around was top of The Hit Parade for several weeks and to be frank we were getting sick of it. We were waiting for something better and could tell that something was in the air. It was 1955 after all!

A poignant image of The Arcade, taken in 2015. Bennetto's Café continues to trade, though all the other businesses have either left or soon would do. The proprietor of the café at the time describes himself as the 'last man standing', his being the last business to close its doors at the end of The Arcade's 117 years as a functioning retail space.

Instead of listening to that old-fashioned stuff, me and my friends soon began listening to Heartbreak Hotel and Don't be Cruel by Elvis Presley on Radio Luxembourg, jiving along as we listened. We loved jiving! On several occasions we were banned from dances at the Town Hall for jiving during the interval.

Teddy boys were 'the pits' to most grown ups. Then it happened! Rock n roll appeared on Auty's list of top ten singles, on display down the arcade! My oh my, apple pie! We became a different species! We dressed differently and we thought differently to everyone else. We were rebels then and we have been rebels ever since!

Dewsbury was a top rock hot spot at the time. Dance Halls were prolific, for example The Ben Riley and The Galleon and numerous other upstairs rooms in and around town. Music meant everything to us, and boyfriends were ditched if they couldn't bop!

Oh, and another thing! Rock n roll is still being done today. I should know. I'm eighty and still rockin!

Part Three
Restoration Dewsbury

13

⚘

Not the Conclusion

There are a number of directories and catalogues of the world's shopping arcades, most of which are seemingly incomplete. The table included within the pages of this chapter was compiled through careful analysis of a sample of these directories and catalogues, as well as through extensive online research. Taken from various sources, the data shows the key information for all arcades built in places with names beginning with C or D and lists approximately 10% of all arcades ever constructed. Despite being less than inspiring in appearance, the table is in fact a mine of information.

Refer to the left-hand column of the table. Notice first the unusually high number of arcades built in Cardiff. Promoted now as the 'City of Arcades', the local authority and tourist bodies rightly make the most of the unique shopping experience that the city offers, even holding an annual 'City of Arcades Week'. The special appeal of arcades for the twenty-first century leisure shopper is duly acknowledged. Notice too the years of construction (shown in the fourth column), many of which fall in the last decade of the nineteenth century, a period of intense provincial arcade building which ended with the opening of The Arcade in Dewsbury.

City/Town	Country	Name	Dates	Status
Cardiff	Wales	Royal	1858-Date	Standing
Cardiff	Wales	Queen St	1866-1987	Demolished
Cardiff	Wales	Morgan	1879-Date	Standing
Cardiff	Wales	High St	1885-Date	Standing
Cardiff	Wales	Andrews	1896-2001?	Demolished
Cardiff	Wales	Wyndham	1896-Date	Standing
Cardiff	Wales	Castle	1897-Date	Standing
Cardiff	Wales	Duke St	1897-Date	Standing
Cardiff	Wales	Dominions	1921-Date	Standing
Cheltenham	England	Montpellier	1832-Date	Standing
Chemnitz	Germany	Arcade	1884-1945	Destroyed
Chester	England	St Michael's	1910-Date	Standing
Chicago	USA	Pullman	1882-1926	Demolished
Cincinnati	USA	Emery	1887-1929	Demolished
Cleveland	USA	Cleveland	1890-Date	Standing
Cleveland	USA	Colonial	1898-Date	Standing
Cologne	Germany	Kon Augusta	1862-1944	Destroyed
Cologne	Germany	Pass Tietz	1902-1944	Destroyed
Cologne	Germany	Stollwerk	1906-1944	Destroyed
Copenhagen	Denmark	Jorcks Pass	1895-Date	Standing
Cremona	Italy	Passage	??-Date	Standing
Danzig	Poland	Passage	Unknown	Destroyed
Derby	England	Strand	1881-Date	Standing
Dewsbury	England	The Arcade	1889-Date	Standing
Doncaster	England	King's	1925-Date	Standing
Dortmund	Germany	Kruger	1916-Date	Standing
Dresden	Germany	Zen Theatre	1898-1945	Destroyed
Dresden	Germany	Konig Albert	1899-1945	Destroyed

Also noticeable is the illustrious company that Dewsbury keeps in the history of arcade construction. Within the same sample are Chicago, Cincinnati, Cleveland, Copenhagen, Danzig and Dortmund. The people of Dewsbury can take pride from their place in the story of this distinctive architectural form. Notice too the number of towns and cities across the UK beginning with the letter D in which arcades were built – just three! You might expect to see a listing for Darlington, Dover, Dundee or Durham. However, it's a mistake to imagine that an arcade was built in every major city and provincial town. On the contrary, they were the exception rather than the rule.

Refer lastly to the right-hand column of the table. Notice the number of arcades that are no longer standing. A quick glance at the preceding dates column will give a clue to the fate of many, destroyed by Allied bombing towards the end of the Second World War: one in Chemnitz, two in Dresden and three in Cologne. Notice also how a number were deliberately demolished. In acts of regrettable urban short-sightedness, some were replaced with inferior replacements or, worse still, soulless modern shopping centres.

The nation's arcades are an important part of our rich architectural heritage. There are endless reasons to preserve, protect and celebrate this rich heritage, though three are especially convincing.

Firstly, the great era of arcade building was relatively short, some 130 years from 1790 to 1920. The peak period of construction from 1860 to 1900 was shorter still. Many have been demolished or destroyed. As a result, arcades are relatively few in number. It's vitally important that we conserve and safeguard those that remain for future generations. Secondly, although it may be impossible to reverse the gradual decline in the fortunes of our town and city centres, it's important not to allow this process to gather pace. Arcades are an attractive feature of many of our town and city centres. In the battle against the onslaught of online shopping, it's crucial that we maintain the allure of each and every enticing aspect of our urban centres. We must give people a reason to go shopping, otherwise they will do it at home in ever greater numbers. Finally, the twenty-first century leisure shopper craves quality, quirky, independent, artisan, creative, alternative options. Anyone can buy anything from the comfort of their kitchen table, and people will continue increasingly to do so. However, it's a mistake to imagine that the yearning for shopping for pleasure is a dying impulse. Millions continue to indulge their desire for leisure shopping every weekend and will continue to do so for decades to come. Arcades are ideally suited to satisfy this demand.

A lesson in keeping faith in, bucking the trend against and maximising the opportunities offered by shopping arcades can be learned close to home – from Leeds! Some of the most elaborate and ornate arcades built towards the end of that great era of arcade building were constructed in Leeds, most notably Frank Matcham's spectacular County Arcade. Opened only a year or so after The Arcade in Dewsbury, and at a time when the rest of Europe was turning against the architectural form, the County Arcade was part of an ambitious redevelopment scheme by the Leeds Estate Company aimed at transforming the eastern side of Briggate. Boasting three circular domes, a glass barrel vault on cast-iron arches and incorporating rich mosaics representing the arts and sciences, the County Arcade was an immediate success, its glazed ceramic tiling from the local Burmantofts factory drawing admirers from far and wide.

Several other arcades were built in the city during a remarkably short period of frenzied construction at either side of the turn of the twentieth century. The arcades of Leeds have continued to be a prized asset for the city throughout the subsequent 120 years or more.

Appropriately, Leeds was one of the last cities to abandon the arcade, building at least two post-war examples: the Empire Arcade in 1961 and Burton's Arcade in 1974, both off Briggate, which could then boast at least seven arcades. Moreover, in 1990 the Briggate arcade network was further extended when a stained-glass roof – the largest in Europe – was erected over Queen Victoria Street to create the Victoria Quarter. Other cities were far behind Leeds in their confidence in arcades, some being content to include pale imitations of arcades into their modern shopping centres, for example the 'arcades' in Gateshead's Metrocentre, Sheffield's Meadowhall and Dartford's Bluewater shopping centres. Leeds has shown admirable faith in the value and benefits of arcades and has reaped an invaluable reward. All the city's arcades have been lovingly restored, not only the County and

Cross Arcades of The Victoria Quarter but also the nearby Queen's, Thornton's and Grand Arcades. The city's shopping arcades are an important factor in the dramatic change in fortunes for the city, which has been transformed for the better and beyond all recognition in the last thirty years.

A telling image of The Arcade, taken not long before the gates were locked for the last time in 2016. The vast majority of the units are vacant, though shoppers can still be seen enjoying a cuppa outside the café at the northern end of The Arcade.

There are only around one hundred arcades still standing in the UK, around fifty having been demolished. Of those still in existence, a significant number are listed buildings, The Arcade in Dewsbury being one of them. The vast majority of those arcades that have protected status are listed at Grade II, the exceptions including London's Royal Opera and Burlington Arcades, which are both listed at Grade I. The architectural value of arcades is thus clearly recognised, as it the need to prevent their numbers dwindling further.

Furthermore, evidence from both close to home and from further afield shows the economic impact that vibrant, visually appealing, faithfully restored shopping arcades can have on the fortunes of our town and city centres. Faced with the onslaught of online shopping, many consumers crave an alternative. Of those who make most of their purchases online, the majority would nevertheless welcome further options to complement their internet shopping. Convenience will never be an alternative to socialising with friends, spending time in a stimulating environment or the delights of window shopping. 'Leisure shoppers', far from a dying breed, are alive and well and itching to be let loose. Arcades are their natural territory.

The Arcade in Dewsbury is an invaluable asset to the town centre. On account of its rich history, and because of the role it could play in a brighter future, it needs to be restored and protected for coming generations.

Bibliography

Arcades: The History of a Building Type - Johann Friedrich Geist   Originally published in 1979 by Prestel-Verlag, Munich

The History and Conservation of Shopping Arcades – Margaret MacKeith   First published in 1986 by Mansell Publishing, London

Shopping Arcades: a gazetteer of extant British Arcades – Margaret MacKeith   First published in 1985 by Mansell Publishing, London

English Shops and Shopping – Kathryn A. Morrison First published in 2003 by Yale University Press, New Haven & London

Printed in Great Britain
by Amazon